DINNER AT NELSON'S

DINNER AT NELSON'S

*Cuisine and Conversation
with the Showbiz Guru*

NELSON ASPEN

NEW HOLLAND

Published in 2011 in Australia by
New Holland Publishers (Australia) Pty Ltd
Sydney • Auckland • London • Cape Town

www.newholland.com.au

1/66 Gibbes Street Chatswood NSW 2067 Australia
218 Lake Road Northcote Auckland New Zealand
86 Edgware Road London W2 2EA United Kingdom
80 McKenzie Street Cape Town 8001 South Africa

National Library of Australia Cataloguing-in-Publication Data:

Aspen, Nelson.

Dinner at Nelson's / Nelson Aspen ; Graeme Gillies, photographer.

ISBN: 9781742570761 (hbk.)

1. Cooking.
2. Dinners and dining.

641.5

Publisher: Linda Williams
Publishing manager: Lliane Clarke
Project editor: Talina McKenzie
Proofreader: Catherine Etteridge
Designer: Emma Gough
Food photography: Graeme Gillies
Dinner setting photography: Emma Gough
Cover photography: Christopher Durham
Chef and styling: Andrew Ballard
Production manager: Olga Dementiev
Printer: Toppan Leefung Printing Limited (China)

Academy Awards ®, Oscars ® and Oscar Night are the registered trademarks and copyrighted property of the
Academy of Motion Picture Arts and Sciences.

Image credits: pp23 (Hollywood star) Kate Ann, (Hollywood Boulevard) David Illif. pp52 (necklace) Tanaka
Who. pp114 (clapper) Matt Batchelor. pp132 (Los Angeles theatre) Chris Eason. pp132 (Broadway sign) Aimée
Tyrrell. pp163 (Hollywood Boulevard sign) Simon Shek. pp.163 (New York Midtown skyline) David Illaf. pp.180
(Brooklyn Bridge) Martin St Amant.

To Mother and Dad,

My two greatest examples of how to entertain and how to be entertain*ing*.

And to Chris, for coming into my life at the perfect time.

A 'BAKER'S DOZEN' DINNER PARTIES

Classic Dishes for Classic Hollywood 19
Dinner with Tony Curtis, Michael Einfeld & Martha Crawford Cantarini

Broccoli Soup, Glazed Carrots, Beef Bourguignon, Zesty Blueberry Angel Food Cake, Sesame Whole Wheat Bread, Election Night Angel Kisses

An Italian Feast in Malibu 35
Dinner with Carol Lynley & Sherry Stringfield

Linguini Pomodoro, Pizza Margarita, Egg-Free Caesar Salad, Vanilla Orange Cookies

Chicken, Canada and Comedy 49
Dinner with Deven Green & Joel Bryant

Celery (Celeriac) Remoulade, Mini-Caprese Appetizers, Chicken Parmesan, Greek Orzo Chicken Bake, Crabby Macaroni and Cheese, Mint Nanaimo Bars

An Aussie Barbecue with American Flavor 65
Dinner with Cameron Daddo and the Pennell Family

Pork Loin with Honey Sauce, Asparagus with Garlic Honey Sauce, Dinner Rolls, Carrot Spice Cake

An Athlete's Choice: Light and Healthy 79
Dinner with Dean Karnazes, Kathrine Switzer, Jared Crouch & Layne Beachley

Simple Salmon Salad, Spinach Lasagna, Eggplant Casserole, Roasted Root Vegetables with Sweet Balsamic Dressing, Jo's Strawberry Rhubarb Pie

Full of Character: Something Different 97
Dinner with Kathryn Joosten & James Arnold Taylor

Shrimp Bisque, Crab Stuffed Mushrooms, Very Veggie Casserole, Irish Stew, Chocolate & Raspberry Cupcakes

Soufflé with the Soap Stars 111
Dinner with the Soap Stars
Gruyere Soufflé, Baked Penne with Ground Beef & Vegetables, Herb Roasted Potatoes, Dodgers Blue-berry Bread Pudding, Lil's Coffee Cake

A Chinese Banquet with Television Greats 129
Dinner with Mindy Cohn, Mimi Kennedy, Alison Arngrim
Vegetarian Hot & Sour Soup, Chicken Fried Rice, Pepper Steak, Shrimp Stir Fry, Cold Sesame Noodles, Quick & Easy Almond Cookies

El Coyote's Mexican Fiesta 145
Dinner with Robert Nisbet & Bonnie Gillespie
Sweet & Savory Steak Salad, Roasted Veggie Salsa, El Coyote's Enchiladas Ranchera, Barb's Almond Toffee Ice Cream Log, Aunt Helen's Anise Cake

A Desperate Housewives Dinner Party 161
Dinner with James & Erin Denton
Nutty Spinach Salad, Bacon-y Green Beans, Baked Salmon Dijon, Bean and Kale Pasta with Sun Dried Tomatoes and Bacon, Elegant Rosemary Cookies

New York, New York! 177
Dinner with Ian Abercrombie & Carolyn Seymour
Cosmo and Champers Cocktails, Lobster Bolognese, Asparagus with Roasted Shallots & Mustard Seeds, Chickpea Pancakes with Spicy Carrots & Oregano Oil, Lemon Verbena Crepes with Strawberries, Christopher's Authentic New York Cheesecake

Limoncello with a Legal Lady and Lassie's Vet 191
Dinner with Jeffrey Werber & Gloria Allred
Veal Ossobucco, My Favorite Meatloaf, Creamy Polenta with Shitake Mushrooms and Manchego Cheese, Lemon Pecan Biscotti, Limoncello

Sunrise Specials 205
Dinner with Ruta Lee & Richard Quest
Walnut Baguette Rounds, Curried Carrot Dip, Garlic Baked Chicken, Philly Cheese Steak Sandwiches, Mel's Fruit Crumble, Sunrise Family Scones

Welcome to the Table!

Food and fitness are such integral parts of my daily life that they always seem to find their way into my reporting... even on the showbiz beat. Whenever I get to appear in studio for TV shows like *Sunrise*, *Brunch*, *Good Morning* or *The Daily Show*, it's always a special treat to share those passions with the audience, be it whipping up some low-fat vegetarian dishes, mixing flavorful cocktails or giving a running tour of some notable location (Hawaii's Diamondhead, the Galway coast in Ireland and a workout-for-pets at Betty White's house spring immediately to mind). Most of my broadcasts, however, are via satellite, and demonstrations are almost impossible when you're stranded in front of a blue screen, only visible from the waist up.

In 2004, my first book *Let's Dish Up a Dinner Party!* was published. Touted as 'a fab guide to entertaining with style', I took readers through the process of putting together the perfect dinner party ... from planning the guest list, all the way through every dining course (Nelson's Succulent Coq au Vin truly is!) and even how to send everyone home at the end of the night safely and satisfied. In 2008, I followed that up with *Hollywood Insider: Exposed!* a dishy celebrity tell-all that merged 'Secrets, Stars & Showbiz.' Of course, there were recipes in that one, too (including an unusually delicious, colorful concoction given to me by the legendary Zsa Zsa Gabor: Vampire Ghoulash!).

I know a lot of people think that throwing a successful dinner party is too much work, pressure, expense, etc. There always seem to be more excuses why not to do it. My best advice to the host-challenged is just to keep it simple!

It always provokes a fun response to ask people 'If you could invite anyone in the world to a dinner party, who would it be?' You'd be surprised how many votes Jesus Christ still gets. And while Justin Bieber may be the most trending topic on Twitter on any given day, I'd still bet that Brangelina and Michelle Obama would top a lot of lists.

After nearly four decades of working in the entertainment industry, I'm lucky enough to have amassed a wide array of trusted friends and colleagues on both sides of the camera. Naturally, that's why I always have the most up-to-date and reliable celebrity news: I am your 'one degree of separation' from all things showbiz! And I will introduce you to dozens of my celeb friends in the pages to follow.

In addition to an assortment of dinner party menus, I've incorporated conversations with some of the very dearest people in my life. These are the folks you would be likely to meet if you did come over to my place for a meal: comedians, athletes, makeup artists, cameramen, journalists, actors and artists. As you might know from my reporting the last two years, I am now bi-coastal and split my residency between Los Angeles and Manhattan. So, one night you might find yourself seated at the giant oak table in my Hollywood Hacienda after cocktails in the garden, overlooking my citrus trees; the next, we might be shoulder-to-shoulder in my gorgeous little pied-a-terre on the Upper West Side of New York City, munching canapés and sipping champagne before heading across the street to the Lincoln Center. Wherever I go, my motto is 'bloom where you're planted!'

So BYOB and belly up to the table. It's time to wine and dine with me and my pals. You are so very welcome!

My Dream Dinner Party

On the pages that follow, you will hear from a lot of fascinating and funny folks. Some names may be new to you, but their insight and experience are sure to entertain. As for the most famous faces of the entertainment industry, I've met and/or interviewed almost all of them... from late great icons such as Gwen Verdon, Glenn Ford and Dixie Carter to current-day idols such as Miley Cyrus, Katie Perry, Kristen Stewart and the Jonas Brothers. But if you were to ask me which mega stars I'd most like to have gathered around my dinner table, this would be my list... all based on personal experience.

HUGH JACKMAN

The first time I interviewed Hugh, I teasingly asked him if it was mandatory that he appear shirtless at least once in every one of his films. Ever the good sport, he laughingly told me, 'It's in my contract!' Well, the truth of the matter is that whenever you run into Hugh, it's likely that he will have a shirt on... and it's apt to be splattered with a bit of magic marker, mustard or other such stain because this guy is, in addition to being the most talented man in showbiz, also the most down-to-earth. We first met at a local mall where he was having lunch with his kids, just being the hands-on devoted dad you'd imagine him to be.

It's impossible not to be a bit starstruck by Hugh Jackman. As multitalented as he is as a performer, he's just as dynamic in 'real life'—whether he's crooning a tune with Catherine Zeta Jones, chatting at a party or just hanging out with his kids. Most celebrities could learn a lot from that guy!

DAME JULIE ANDREWS

Having interviewed the divine Dame a couple times in traditional press junket situations, I was excited to score an exclusive half-hour one-on-one with this legendary leading lady to celebrate the release of her autobiography *Home*. Even better was getting to hang out together in her smartly appointed Manhattan hotel suite for nearly an hour and a half!

A proper English tea party was laid out for us, and we sipped PG Tips but skipped the scones! She's a gracious, gorgeous hostess and as interested as she is interesting when it comes to conversation. She has a great saying we should all remember: 'Perseverance is failing nineteen times and succeeding the twentieth.' We laughed and gabbed about our mutual friends, favorite Broadway musicals and even sang a few bars together. Wow!

MERYL STREEP

She is every bit as marvelous you can imagine, as regal and elegant as you'd expect movie royalty to be, but with such cognizance and humor about this crazy industry that she keeps remarkably grounded. She knows she's revered, so she just relaxes and enjoys it!

I spoke to her recently about her award-winning turn as Julia Child in *Julie & Julia*. Knowing she had taken some culinary technique classes in preparation for the film, I had to ask her for a demonstration of making the perfect omelet. She had just begun to explain the required wrist action when I reached into my bag of tricks and pulled out my own piece of prized cookware: an omelet pan given to me more than a quarter of a century ago by my mentor, the late, great soap opera star Mary Stuart. ('Every bachelor should know how to make an omelet,' Mary wisely told me!)

'Would you mind showing me?' I asked the multi-Oscar-winning Meryl. Without missing a beat, she grabbed the pan and gave me a perfect lesson. Not many A-listers would be so quick and happy to play along. It is impossible not to adore her.

LEONARDO DICAPRIO

I have such a history with Leo that I devoted an entire chapter to him in my last book. From being a TV show's designated 'Leo reporter' and co-hosting a documentary on his life to interviewing him several times and befriending his effervescent mom, Irmalin, he's certainly one of my favorite leading men.

I admit he had to win me over. As much as I loved *Titanic*, I dismissed him as a 'heartthrob'. But look at the amazing work he's exhibited since then! *Blood Diamond*, *Revolutionary Road*, *The Departed* and *Shutter Island* are especially high on my list.

He never fails to remember me with a smile, well wishes and courtesy. Good-humored, smart and considerate. That's good enough to be A-list in my book, even without his massive box-office appeal!

SALMA HAYEK

This extremely talented actress and producer is certainly on the A-list in Hollywood, but that doesn't mean she wouldn't fit right in a dinner party.

I'd always found her an appealing public figure, but when I was waiting to interview her she proved what a great gal she must be. I was in a media holding area where I spent several hours with other journalists, waiting for our designated appointment with Ms Hayek. It was morning, so there was a catering table filled with urns of coffee, fruit platters, baskets of breads and even an omelet bar. A long line of camera crew and reporters queued up for their breakfasts and all of a sudden Salma appeared and took her place in the back of the line, waiting patiently for her turn to tuck in to the goodies. There she was, a tiny little goddess—picture perfect with hair, makeup and wardrobe—happily hanging out with the rest of us to grab a bite to eat before the cameras rolled. I was very impressed.

Salma may live the high life of a glamorous star, but she also strikes me as a lot of fun just to hang around with! Doesn't she sound perfect to include at the table?

ZAC EFRON

Few young stars impress me with smarts and manners. I first met Zac Efron when he was promoting *Hairspray* ... before the Fame Train hit him full speed. He struck me as an energetic, playful kid who was having an awfully good time enjoying the ride. But after the global phenomenon of the *High School Musical* franchise, I worried that 'Famous Person's Disease' may have infected him. Now—meeting him again at the ripe old age of 23—I find him to be self-effacing, friendly and gregarious. Polite and courteous to everyone around him (when the cameras were rolling and especially when they were not). We chatted about how he handles fame, the choices he makes in his career and a little bit about our mutual love of baseball, too!

I mentioned to Zac that some people have said that, if he continues the way he's going, he could be the next Tom Hanks. He was surprised and delighted with that. After all, even movie stars can use a good role model!

ANGELINA JOLIE

I've only met her once (and had to jump through hoops just to secure that all-too-brief interview), but I find her such a unique and intriguing character among the multitude of other celebrities that I'd absolutely want her to come by for dinner! I've had considerably more first-hand experience with Brad, so he can stay home and babysit their brood while Angie enjoys a night out!

Angelina does more good for the world than a stadium full of Lindsays and Britneys. And she does it all while continuing to deliver great screen performances and red-carpet glamour! I can only assume it's schadenfreude that makes for all the nasty, unauthorized biographies and tabloid reports against her.

And you know what? She's such a humanitarian, I bet she'd even help with the dishes!

TOM CRUISE

For our first meeting, Tom's handlers had a not-uncommon assortment of requirements. Unlike some journalists who feel restricted by conditions, I believe that any reporter worth his salt can still conduct an interesting and revealing interview without causing strife. I knew that he and I shared a mutual fascination with the story of World War II German resistance, so I brought along a signed copy of my book on the subject, *Sacred Blood*. When I entered the room, he did something almost no other celebrity does: he stood up to introduce himself and shake hands. When I gave him the book, he was so surprised and appreciative that he delayed the cameras rolling for several minutes so he could find out more about my background with the subject matter.

I left the room feeling like I'd had one of my very best interviews. Few stars of that caliber take the effort to make a reporter feel that special. A cynic might say it was all an act, but while there's no discounting Tom's magnetic media savvy, I believe he's a rare example of 'what you see if what you get'—whether that means jumping on a couch, being playful with his kids or having an off-camera gab with me about a shared interest.

VIGGO MORTENSEN

Viggo is not only a consummate actor (my number one), he's a poet and linguist. The two times I've interviewed him, he's impressed me with his thoughtful answers, impressive vocabulary and compelling eye contact. He's a gentleman to everyone around him and definitely subscribes to the policy of treating others they way he'd prefer to be treated.

He and I both started our careers in the mid-1980s, working on the same soap opera, *Search for Tomorrow*. But (as we all did) he also worked odd jobs to make ends meet, such as bartending and waiting tables. Maybe that's what's kept him unaffected by 'Famous Person's Disease.' In fact, he initially was going to turn down *The Lord of the Rings* trilogy because it would mean spending too much time away from his young son, Henry. However, it was Henry—a fan of the books—who convinced him to accept the role of Aragorn. Of course, fame followed.

GOLDIE HAWN

Dynamic, dynamite Goldie and I used to hang out at the same fitness studio when I first moved to LA many years ago.

We reunited to do a very in-depth feature on an educational program she helped to create through her foundation. It was great to see a more serious, thoughtful side to the Emmy and Oscar winner. From her body of film work, we're used to seeing her as the perpetually adorable, giggly bubblehead, but she's actually as brainy as she is beautiful.

It's always fun to connect with a celebrity whose body of work you greatly admire. For generations, she's been bringing laughter and love to fans all around the world. It's especially wonderful when that star turns out to be the kind of person you'd like to have as a friend.

ADAM SANDLER

I know a lot of reporters who have had a tough time getting Adam to warm up in interviews, but when I met him for a chat, he was exceedingly warm, bright and ... oh, yeah ... funny! ('ribald' would be a good adjective!)

A year before I met Adam, his production company Happy Madison invaded my neighborhood for a long location shoot for his film *Bedtime Stories*. Sandler's company not only notified us well in advance, they were all clean and courteous. Around-the-clock security was in place for the late night and early morning goings-on To top it all off, every household was gifted with an elaborate 'thank you' gift basket of gourmet treats after filming had wrapped.

I thought that was very classy and when I finally met Adam in 2010, I told him so. As the executive producer of a huge filmmaking division, he told me how much he appreciated the feedback. Class act.

Wash Up!
It's Time for Dinner!

We're about to launch into a series of dinner party menus I have assembled from my own personal collection. I'm a pretty simple cook when it comes to what I enjoy making and serving, so you should find these easy to execute. I do, however, encourage you to personalize them to your own tastes and dietary restrictions. I even make suggestions for wine pairings but I don't pretend to be an expert on that subject ... I just love wine! I made sure to consult with my 'cork dork' buddy David Organisak to come up with suggestions. (Check him out at www.vinologue.blogspot. com.) I always tell my friends in New Zealand that I've never met a Kiwi I didn't like. And I've never tasted a Kiwi wine I didn't love!

A few tips and reminders...

Like Howard Hughes and Ashton Kutcher (believe it or not), I'm an admitted clean freak and can't wash my hands often enough. Err on the side of caution, especially when handling food, and keep yourself and your work surfaces disinfected by washing up often with hot, soapy water. 'Clean as you go' is a motto of mine. It also makes the end-of-the-evening ritual of tidying up go much faster!

Just as your hands and counters should be immaculate, so should your dishes, glasses, napkins and flatware. Take the time to make sure everything on the table sparkles! Your guests may not notice the attention you give to those details, but you can bet they would if you didn't!

Have a look around your home. Is everything neat and tidy? Make sure the cat litter box has been changed, the floors vacuumed and the pillows fluffed. Inspect the bathroom and make sure there's plenty of soap, hand towels and toilet paper. (Have a look at what's in your medicine chest: you can be sure some nosy guests will!)

I even go outside and enter the house or apartment as if I'm one of my own guests. Is the entranceway swept and inviting? Make it as welcoming as possible, perhaps with pots of colorful, fragrant flowers or votive candles. Remember, 'you never get a second chance to make a first impression!'

If you have kids or pets, make sure they don't assault your guests upon their arrival. Create a relaxing environment, from the lighting to your choice of music. If the attendees are friends of yours, why not put out some favorite photographs of them in the living room? I'll bet it's been a while since you swapped out any of the shots in your picture frames.

If your guests bring you a gift, make a fuss over it. If it's a wine, offer to serve it with dinner—don't be a slave to your agenda. Flexibility is the sign of a gracious host. (Being a dinner party host isn't much different from being a television host… just be welcoming, warm, prepared and a good listener!)

Going with the flow isn't always easy—believe me, I know. But a dinner party is about enjoying yourself, not stressing out over minutiae. So what if some guests are running late or they accidentally drop one of your crystal champagne flutes? Heck, you can even burn the main course and it's not really the end of the world. Laugh about it. The real reason you're having the party is to enjoy the pleasure of each other's company. With a little forethought and attention to detail, your evening will probably come off without a hitch.

The very best advice I can give you for throwing a dinner party can best be summed up by quoting the inimitable Noel Coward's comment on Joan Crawford's skills at entertaining: 'Joan not only gives a party … she goes to it!'

Enjoy yourself!

Michael Einfeld

Martha Crawford
Cantarini

Tony Curtis

Classic Dishes
for Classic Hollywood

Dinner with

Tony Curtis
Michael Einfeld
Martha Crawford Cantarini

Menu

Broccoli Soup
Glazed Carrots
Beef Bourguignon
Zesty Blueberry Angel Food Cake
Cosmo and Champers Cocktails
Election Night Angel Kisses

Suggested Wine

Pinot Noir

AUTHOR'S NOTE: *Film icon Tony Curtis passed away not long after completing this conversation for the dinner party you are about to enjoy. In addition to the tremendous body of motion picture work that will be his legacy, he will be remembered for his humor, elan and artistry (he was an accomplished painter) ... much of which comes through in the pages to follow.*

Silver screen legend Tony Curtis was born Bernard Schwarz in the Depression-era Bronx borough of New York City. After serving in the Marines, he enrolled in acting school and brought his boyish good looks to Hollywood, where he was snapped up by Universal Studios and given a seven-year contract. Paying his dues with various bit parts, he hit his stride co-starring with Kirk Douglas in *Spartacus* and then went on to stardom with films like *The Vikings*, *The Defiant Ones*, *The Great Race* and the classic *Some Like it Hot*, opposite Jack Lemmon and Marilyn Monroe. He even has the

I asked Tony if there was any role he regrets missing out on. With his characteristic good humor, he answered, 'Any movie that I wasn't in, was a loss.' What about being star struck? Had he ever been? 'What time is it?' he laughs. 'Yes, it started with Cary Grant and it hasn't stopped yet.'

pop culture distinction of playing himself (as Stony Curtis) on the cartoon comedy *The Flintstones*. A sixty-year film career, a tumultuous Tinseltown private life (he is currently married to his sixth wife) and countless accolades haven't slowed him down a bit. In fact, he recently inked a deal to co-star with Sigourney Weaver and Alicia Silverstone in the new Amy Heckerling film *Vamps*. He's really a national treasure! I remember when I first came to Hollywood, I used to see him holding court at the popular Le Dome restaurant on the Sunset Strip, always surrounded by a bevy of beauties. What a star to behold! He now lives outside of Las Vegas, but returns to Hollywood often for work. I was introduced to him through his manager, Michael Einfeld.

Michael and I have known each other so long we can't even remember how we met! I do recall it was around the time he had helped propel Hilary Swank to stardom. Like me, he commutes between Los Angeles and Manhattan (which ironically doesn't make it any easier to catch up with each other), and manages a vast array of actors, dancers and choreographers ranging from soap stars to veterans like Tony, Tina Louise and Shirley Jones. He's a dynamo, personally and professionally, and hysterically funny.

Michael told me he first met Tony through a publicist friend. 'Tony was with a big agency and not being handled well. I had other older stars, so we had lunch and totally hit it off. Within two weeks, I had two jobs for him and we've been together ever since. He's the classiest guy in show business. He's a *mensch* (Yiddish slang for 'great guy')! Some people are difficult but he's not. He'll do a job and give me extra commission ... did you ever hear of such a thing?'

The team of Tony and Michael work well together, although as you'll see ... one is wonderfully verbose and the other a man of few words! I admire them both.

In the Hollywood of the 1940s and 50s, horse trainer/show rider Martha Crawford Cantarini was the most sought-after stuntwoman in the movie business, and a regular stunt double for leading ladies such as Eleanor Parker, Anne Baxter and Shirley MacLaine. She schmoozed with almost all of the greats of the silver screen: Gregory Peck, Clark Gable, Glenn Ford, Joseph Cotten, Claudette Colbert, Yvonne Decarlo and many others. After her long film career, ranging from features like *Love Me Tender* and *The Big Country*, Martha (along with her horse Frosty) hosted a TV show in the 1960s before retiring to British Columbia. She was honored with the Golden Boot Award and was inducted into the Hollywood Stuntmen's Hall of Fame. After I reviewed her marvelous autobiography, *Fall Girl*, she reached out to me via email and we became pen pals. She's a charming lady and a wonderful tie to the long-lost glamour and excitement of Hollywood's bygone era.

Michael on his client, Tony Curtis: 'He's passionate about what he does. It's not about being famous for him. He's an actor's actor. He loves discovering a character. He can take a mediocre scene and turn it into something fantastic, active and alive! The man has a twinkle in his eye and star charisma.' And who would he choose to be Tony's perfect leading lady? 'Shirley Jones. Because

Who would be Michael's dream client to snare? 'Bernadette Peters. My first job in LA was interning on a movie called Pink Cadillac *starring Clint Eastwood. I had to get tapes on actresses for him to consider. Bernadette, Melanie Griffith and Geena Davis were all up for a part. He passed on everybody. So I kept sending in different Bernadette Peters tapes and finally he called and said, "I think I want to meet that Bernadette Peters" and that was that. Isn't it crazy? And I've never met her!'*

I represent her, too!' Tony responds, 'I did it with my heart and soul. And I kissed every leading lady I could.' (There is that twinkle!)

Then I have to ask Martha, 'If Tony had tried to kiss you, would you have let him?' Laughing, she comes back with, 'Tony, no! Nice guy, but the slick ones are not my type. Elvis Presley, yes! He winked at me once and I haven't recovered yet!' That's no faint praise … she and he became pals on the set of *Love Me Tender*, although she admits that she finds Jeff Bridges to be the most 'swoon-worthy' star of today.

In addition to being a star of the first magnitude, Tony also enjoyed a long tenure as a sex symbol. In his esteem, 'a celebrity is someone who brings to his profession a truth and compassion.' And as for the status of heartthrob? He dismisses that and thinks that what's really sexy is 'allowing yourself the privilege of bringing truth and compassion.'

After being around show business for so long, how have these pros seen it change? Tony says, 'The major change has been that Hollywood has lost its way. An actor must now consider all of the aspects about what his job may entail. Television has forced actors to work with a sense of urgency, they must come up with the "gift" of acting with very little time to their advantage.'

'Someone like me would starve to death these days because of all the computer generated effects,' Martha laments. 'Today's stunt persons have to be far more versatile than I was—do everything!'

For Michael, 'It's hugely different since I started in the late 1980s. Everything happens faster now because of technology. So much is done with the push of a button. It's also much less personal and around-the-clock. Everything's email, which is handy but you're typing and not talking. In the old days, you had to talk! There are fewer projects now, too, since the economy tanked. They're paying less with budget cuts as well.' Still, I can't imagine Michael ever doing anything else!

(L-R) Michael Einfeld.

Broccoli Soup

4 tablespoons olive oil
½ onion, sliced
1 garlic clove, sliced
1 medium potato, diced into small cubes
3 heads of broccoli, cut into small florets
41/4 cups (2 pints, 1 L) vegetable stock
1¼ cup (10 fl oz, 300ml) cream
salt and pepper
pinch of nutmeg
2 tablespoons toasted almonds, sliced

Place the olive oil, onions, garlic and potatoes into a saucepan over medium heat.
Stir and heat for a few minutes until garlic and onions soften. Add broccoli.
Stir in the stock and cream, seasoning to taste with salt, pepper and nutmeg. Simmer for 10 minutes.
Remove from heat.

Once cooled, ladle the soup in batches into a blender. Put the lid on, leaving enough space for the steam to escape. Puree until it becomes smooth, then pour back into the saucepan and stir occasionally until piping hot. Add more cream if desired, for consistency.

Serve with the sliced almonds as garnish.

I grew up on a farm and had a beautiful Shetland pony named Winston (after my parents' brand of cigarette, if you can fathom that!). Sometimes, especially if we had guests my father wanted to impress, he would bring Winston right into the kitchen, off the adjacent porch, and let him drink warm coffee out of a saucer. It always brings a smile to my face to remember the incongruous sight of that docile equine standing at the kitchen table! Of course, my mother was duly horrified. I wondered if Martha had a similar experience with any of the horses she'd been close to over the years. 'My horse, Frosty, used to stand with his head in my kitchen window over the sink as I did the dishes!' Maybe a horse in the kitchen isn't such a crazy idea after all... as long as they're house trained!

Glazed Carrots

This is so ridiculously easy, you might feel guilty. Then again, you might just appreciate having something so simple (yummy and pretty, too!) that you are free to concentrate on a more elaborate main dish!

2½ cups (20oz, 600gm) carrots, sliced diagonally
2 tablespoons butter
2 tablespoons brown sugar
1 teaspoon orange peel, grated
½ teaspoon salt

Cook the carrots in hot water or a steamer until they are tender. Drain.

Melt the butter in a large saucepan or skillet over medium heat.
Add the cooked carrots, then stir in the sugar, grated orange peel and salt.
Continue stirring constantly until carrots are glazed.

Beef Bourguignon

4 lb (2 kg) beef rump or chuck, cut into 1in (2.5cm) cubes
⅓ cup (2½ fl oz, 70 ml) warm cognac
2 whole onions
2 cloves garlic
1 teaspoon thyme
1 bay leaf
4 cups (1 pint, 950 ml) dry red wine
1 tablespoon salt
1 teaspoon black pepper
1 slice orange
2 tablespoons butter
18 small white onions, peeled

- -

Preheat oven to 300°F (150°C).

Heat a large oven-safe baking dish over medium-high heat. Add beef and brown thoroughly on all sides.
Pour warm cognac over beef and ignite with a match. Allow flames to burn out.

Add 2 whole onions, garlic, thyme, bay leaf, wine, salt, pepper and orange slice.
Bring to a boil on top of the range. Cover dish and place in oven. Bake for 2 hours, turning once or twice.

After 2 hours, melt butter in a skillet. Add small white onions and brown. Add to the beef in the baking dish
and cook for 30 minutes more. Remove beef and onions to a hot serving platter.
Reduce the liquid before adding the beef and onions back in. Stir and serve.

Zesty Blueberry Angel Food Cake

I love angel food cake. Plain, simple and virtually fat-free, so it's a dessert I can eat without guilt when I'm marathon training (those distance runs eat up the sugar and carbs). You can serve it with almost any kind of sweet topping or side, but I like it simple... like this version with lemon and blueberries. Experiment and create your own signature version!

1½ cups (12oz, 350gm) sugar (divided, see below)
1 cup (8oz, 240gm) flour
12 large egg whites
1¼ teaspoons cream of tartar
½ teaspoon salt
1 teaspoon vanilla extract
1½ cups (12oz, 350gm) fresh or frozen blueberries
2 tablespoons flour
1 tablespoon grated lemon zest
(Optional) glaze:
1 cup (8oz, 240gm) powdered sugar (icing sugar)
3 tablespoons lemon juice

- -

Preheat oven to 375°F (190°C).

Sift together ½ cup (4oz, 120gm) sugar and 1 cup (8oz, 240gm) flour.
In a large bowl, beat egg whites with a mixer until they foam.
Add cream of tartar and salt; beat until soft peaks form. Gradually add 1 cup (8oz, 240gm) sugar, beating until peaks stiffen. Gradually sift flour mixture over egg white mixture, folding in.
Next, fold in vanilla and berries.

Combine 2 additional tablespoons of flour and lemon zest. Sprinkle over egg white mixture, then fold.

Spoon batter into ungreased 10in (25cm) tube pan, spreading evenly.
Press through batter with a butter knife to break up any air pockets.

Bake for 40 minutes or until cake becomes spongy to a light touch.
Remove from oven and turn pan upside down until completely cooled.
Loosen cake from pan using butter knife or narrow metal spatula, then invert onto cake dish.

For a lemony glaze, whisk powdered sugar and lemon juice in a small bowl, then drizzle over cake.

Classic Dishes for Classic Hollywood

Sesame Whole Wheat Bread

Here's a great recipe my mom taught me. She and I are both bread fanatics and this one is sooo good slathered in butter, or to get that last bit of gravy off your plate after a meal!

4 cups (2lb, 950gm) wholewheat (wholemeal) flour
2 cups (16oz, 480gm) all purpose flour (plain flour)
¾ cup (6oz, 180gm) sugar
2 teaspoons salt
¼ cup (2oz, 60gm) toasted sesame seeds
4 cups (2 pints, 950ml) buttermilk
4 teaspoons baking soda

- -

Preheat oven to 375°F (190°C).

Stir together flours, sugar, salt and sesame seeds in a large bowl.

In a separate bowl, combine buttermilk and baking soda, then stir into flour mixture.

Pour into 2 x greased 9 x 5 x 3in (23 x 12 x 7.5cm) loaf pans. Reduce oven temperature to 350°F (180°C).

Place pans in oven and bake for 1 hour. Remove from pans to cool on rack.

Election Night Angel Kisses

Every four years, whether they wanted to or not, my parents threw a Presidential Election Night party, with lots of patriotic decorations and a ballot box for all their (mostly Republican) guests to cast a vote as they entered the front door. TVs and radios in every room covered the ongoing election and it was always an exciting and festive night, regardless of your political affiliation. This is Mom's recipe for three dozen delicious, sweet treats to have on the banquet table.

2 egg whites
½ teaspoon cream of tartar
⅛ teaspoon salt
1 teaspoon vanilla extract
¾ cup (6oz, 180gm) superfine sugar (caster sugar)
½ cup (4oz, 120gm) chocolate chips
½ cup (4oz, 120gm) chopped nuts

- -

Preheat oven to 300°F (150°C).

Beat egg whites, cream of tartar and salt in a small bowl until peaks form. Add vanilla.
Add sugar, gradually, beating until stiff. Fold in chocolate chips and nuts.

Drop teaspoons of mixture 2in (5cm) apart on ungreased brown wrapping paper, laid on a cookie sheet.
Bake until dry (about 25 minutes).

Let cool slightly before removing from paper. Set on rack to cool completely before storing in an airtight jar.

Carol Lynley

Sherry Stringfield

An Italian Feast in Malibu

Dinner with

Carol Lynley
Sherry Stringfield

Menu

Linguini Pomodoro
Pizza Margarita
Caesar Salad
Vanilla Orange Cookies

Suggested Wine

Chianti or Chianti Reserva

Carol Lynley has the distinction of being 'my favorite movie star.' Like millions of other adolescent boys in the 1960s and 1970s, I fell in love with her onscreen image the first time I saw the greatest of all disaster flicks, *The Poseidon Adventure*. The willowy blonde in the hippie fringe vest, hot pants and go-go boots captivated me and I became an ardent fan. Whenever I see the film again, I stand by my assertion that she was the greatest beauty of her time. That perfect bone structure from her combined Irish and American Indian roots, those enormous blue eyes and the coquettish tilt of her head… heaven! We met when I was 15 years old and wound up becoming lifelong friends. Now in her sixties, she still conveys the image of the ultimate 'California Girl' (even though she was born and raised in New York City!): sun-kissed, laid back and living right on the Malibu shoreline.

Sherry Stringfield is, for my money, the most naturally beautiful woman in contemporary Hollywood. I'd first become aware of her work when she debuted on the long running soap opera *Guiding Light*, playing an unscrupulous bad girl named Blake Thorpe. After a few years, she chose to pursue a career in primetime and became a star on the long running medical drama *ER*, playing Dr Susan Lewis. Multiple Emmy and Golden Globe nominations followed.

On being cast as glamorous vixen 'Blake,' Sherry said it couldn't have been further from her own persona. 'I'd just graduated from college and had all-one-length hippie hair almost down to my waist. Wash and go wild hair! I wore cowboy boots, jeans and t-shirts. That's the person who auditioned for an all glitz 'n' glam soap opera and a week later they were chopping my hair off and putting a shoulder-padded jacket on me. I've had all those different looks over the years and it cracks me up. People don't usually recognize me, but when they do, they say "Oh, my God… you're so not that!"'

(L-R) Beautiful inside and out, Carol Lynley and Sherry Stringfield

It was my great honor to bring these two wonderful women together for a lunch in Malibu at one of Carol's favorite Italian joints, Giovanni's. They'd never met, but I had a feeling they'd hit it off, and indeed they did. Carol even brought her the gift of a book and we lingered at our table for hours, the conversation never letting up for a minute. All three of us were long-time single folks at the time, so we pondered Carol's observation that 'Marriage is for people who are afraid of life.' After a couple glasses of good wine, that seemed *really* deep and we bantered on and on with our own often comical war stories on the subject.

These are the three dishes we enjoyed that fantastic afternoon at Giovanni's, adapted to my own cooking style for you to enjoy. Serve all three simultaneously and enjoy grazing 'family style'. And while I recommend a good Italian chianti to accompany your meal, we were perfectly content with our (bottles of) chardonnay! Don't be a slave to rules when it comes to wine pairings—drink what you like.

Carol, herself an accomplished cook, says that many of the best meals she's enjoyed have been prepared by some of the men she's dated ... including British actor Oliver Reed and the one-and-only Frank Sinatra (of course, she still refers to him by the name he used in his inner circle: 'Francis Albert')! It isn't widely known that he enjoyed making meals at home and expertly prepared Sicilian dishes. 'When he wanted to let friends know to come over, he'd call them on the telephone and when they'd answer, he'd start the blender so they'd know he was making drinks!'

She taught herself the art of Chinese cooking, but she still likes to go out for Asian fare. And it paid off when she finally got to meet one of the acting peers she'd always loved: Sir Anthony Hopkins. 'I was at a Chinese restaurant in Malibu. I went over to say how much I admired him and I was suddenly speechless! He was very sweet about it. He was lovely and I just made a fool of myself. I kept hugging him and I kept apologizing. People don't like to be hugged by strangers, you know,' she laughs.

Aside from the shared experience of being lovely leading ladies, Carol and Sherry also know what it's like to be single mothers, supporting their kids by working in the daunting and unstable world of show business. Carol, even

> *It's always interesting to find out how different casting might have affected a movie. Imagine if Bette Davis had played Scarlett O'Hara in* Gone With The Wind, *rather than pitch-perfect Vivien Leigh? Carol dismisses that she was in serious contention to play Faye Dunaway's Bonnie Parker in* Bonnie and Clyde, *but does admit to having turned down Susan Anspach's role in* Five Easy Pieces. *She also had to turn down Roman Polanski's offer to star as the unraveling, sexually repressed beauty in his brilliant 1965 piece* Repulsion. *She was busy shooting another film, so Polanski had to settle for Catherine Deneuve ... but named the character after Carol, in tribute.*

with over fifty films on her resume, turned frequently to television projects in the 1970s and 1980s and credits the popular series *Fantasy Island* for helping to put her daughter through college. She starred in the original pilot movie and was, in fact, the most frequent guest star to Ricardo Montalban's magical isle on the studio back lot from 1978 to 1984. She jokes that any time a celebrity called in sick, producer Aaron Spelling would have her fill the part. From a murderess society girl, to a high-class hooker, to a broken down ballerina, 'I did every fantasy at least twice!'

For Sherry, raising two young children in Los Angeles is often frustrating. 'In the grocery store at my nine-year-old's eye level are all these magazines with women's hoochies right in front of her.' But, she concedes, 'What's great about LA is being able to be outdoors so much. We'd live outside in a tent if we could! We ride horses, play sports. I give them a sense of their own freedom before it's taken away by the "thought police". I want them to have free minds and free hearts. Nurturing those qualities in a positive way is great. As a parent, you do what you can. I'm pretty strict. They're not even on the internet! I'm old school.'

I ask her, 'What are you going to do when they grow up and want to go to a party at Paris Hilton's house?' She screams, 'Omigod! Omigod! I have no idea! I haven't even thought of that!'

We all laugh and fill up our wine glasses!

Linguini Pomodoro

Succulent tomato sauce is the key to this delish, simple dish. Make sure your tomatoes are gorgeously ripe and in season. Penne and fusilli are the most popular pastas for this recipe because of the way they hold the sauce, but Carol likes linguini. Use whatever kind you fancy! She also swears that the intense garlic will cure any stuffy sinuses (but if this is too garlicky for you, by all mean modify to suit your individual taste). This is a generous recipe but leftovers are great cold or reheated the next day.

4 cups (2 lb, 950gm) ripe tomatoes, cored and roughly chopped
4 tablespoons olive oil
salt and black pepper to taste
4 garlic cloves, finely chopped
1 cup (8oz, 240gm) fresh basil leaves, finely chopped
2 lb (1 kg) pasta
Parmesan cheese

While boiling the salted water for pasta, place the tomatoes, oil, salt, pepper, garlic and ½ cup (4oz, 120gm) of the basil into a bowl. Use a fork to press these ingredients together well.
When the pasta water is boiling, add the pasta.

As the pasta cooks, ladle approximately (depending on the thickness you desire) 1 cup (8oz, 240gm) of the starchy water to the tomato mixture and stir well.

Drain pasta when it is al dente and place in a large serving bowl. Toss it with the sauce.
Top with the other ½ cup (4oz, 120gm) of basil and lots of fresh, grated Parmesan cheese.

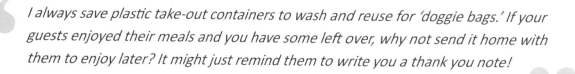

I always save plastic take-out containers to wash and reuse for 'doggie bags.' If your guests enjoyed their meals and you have some left over, why not send it home with them to enjoy later? It might just remind them to write you a thank you note!

Pizza Margarita

I like to make this delicious, classic pizza to serve instead of bread with my pasta dishes and salads. It's also a great snack. I don't consider it cheating to use store-bought pizza dough. It's a great time saver and often turns out better than dough I could make myself, anyway!

If you decide to serve this to accompany the linguine pomodoro and Caesar salad, prep it a few hours in advance and stick it in the fridge until it's time to bake; one less thing you will have to be bothered with at mealtime!

Sauce
1 tablespoon olive oil
½ red onion, diced
4 tablespoons garlic, minced
salt and black pepper to taste
6 fresh basil leaves, chopped
3 tablespoons red wine
1 x 14oz can (1½ cups, 400gm) whole plum tomatoes

Pizza
premade pizza dough
¼ cup (2oz, 60gm) chopped tomatoes
1 teaspoon dried oregano
fresh basil
fresh mozzarella cheese, sliced thinly

Preheat oven to 450°F (230°C).

Heat the oil in a pot over medium heat. Add onion and garlic and cook for 5–7 minutes, or until onions are translucent. Season with salt and pepper to taste and add the basil leaves, wine, tomatoes and ½ cup (4fl oz, 120ml) water. Bring to a boil and simmer for 20–25 minutes.

Ladle sauce onto pizza dough and spread over top, leaving a 1in (2.5cm) border on the edge. Top with the tomatoes, oregano, some basil leaves and mozzarella slices.

Bake until crust is golden and the cheese has melted, about 12–14 minutes. Cut into wedges and serve immediately.

This classic Italian pizza was named for Italy's beloved Queen Margherita, who reigned in the late 19th century. She enjoyed eating the flatbread pizza of the common people, much to the consternation of her court. She summoned Chef Rafaelle Esposito from his pizzeria in Naples to her palace, where he created this version in tribute to the sovereign ... and the Italian flag: the tomatoes, cheese and basil represent the national colors of red, white and green! When you eat margarita pizza, you're enjoying a tasty slice of Italian culture. Molto bene!

Egg-Free Caesar Salad

While one of the most popular salads in the world, a lot of people seem to take issue with the idea of raw eggs and/or anchovies. So this version skips the eggs altogether and goes easy on the anchovies (plus, if you mince them well you will get their flavor without the consistency some folks dislike).

2 garlic cloves, halved
3 tablespoons olive oil
1 tablespoons fresh lemon juice
1 teaspoon lime juice
1 tablespoon minced anchovies
dash of Worcestershire sauce
salt and black ground pepper
2 heads romaine lettuce, washed and dried
croutons (I like to crumble up a day-old baguette)
1 cup (8oz, 240gm) Parmesan cheese, grated

Rub the inside of your salad bowl with the garlic and discard the cloves.
Whisk together the oil and juices, then stir in the anchovies and dash of Worcestershire.
Season with salt and pepper to taste.

Tear the lettuce into pieces and place in bowl. Pour dressing over the top and toss.
Top with croutons and cheese, then toss again.

Most people incorrectly assume that the Caesar salad was named for the Roman emperor, but it's more accurately attributed to an Italian-born Mexican restaurateur named Caesar Cardini. His daughter claims that he invented the recipe in 1924 out of necessity—working with the only leftover ingredients he had in his kitchen on a public holiday!

Vanilla Orange Cookies

Growing up with Creamsicles as my favorite ice cream treat, the combination of orange and vanilla is still one of my favorite tastes. Here is a dandy recipe I adapted from a cooking blog. If you care to get a little fancy and add vanilla icing, they'd be especially nice for a holiday party ... but I like 'em just like this!

2½ cups (20oz, 600gm) all-purpose flour (plain flour)

¾ teaspoon baking soda

½ teaspoon salt

1 cup (8oz, 240gm) butter, softened

½ cup (4oz, 120gm) sugar

½ cup (4oz, 120gm) brown sugar, packed

1 large egg

1 teaspoon vanilla extract

$\frac{1}{8}$ teaspoon almond extract

2 tablespoons orange zest

2 cups (16oz, 480gm) vanilla chips (or white chocolate chips, if unavailable. Add 1 extra teaspoon vanilla extract.)

- -

Preheat oven to 375°F (190°C).

In a small bowl, combine flour, baking soda and salt; set aside.

In a large bowl, cream butter and sugars until light and creamy.

Beat in egg, vanilla and almond extracts until smooth.

Gradually add flour mixture until combined. Stir in orange zest and chips.

Drop rounded spoonfuls onto ungreased cookie sheets.

Bake for 8–10 minutes or until golden brown around edges.

Cool on sheets before transferring to rack to cool completely. Store in an airtight container.

Deven Green

Joel Bryant

Chicken, Canada and Comedy

Dinner with

Deven Green
Joel Bryant

Menu

Celery Remoulade
or
Mini-Caprese Appetizers
Chicken Parmesan
or
Greek Orzo Chicken Bake
Mint Nanaimo Bars

Suggested Wine

Coppola's Bianco Pinot Grigio or
light-bodied red such as
Georges Duboeuf's Fleurie

Deven Green and Joel Bryant, an LA-based, award-winning comedy duo, are a married couple who became very dear friends of mine long before we ever met, courtesy of the internet! Like millions of others, I'd discovered Deven's brilliant parody videos that were sweeping YouTube and winning all sorts of new media and comedy accolades. I couldn't help but drop her a message of praise and appreciation. Like the gracious star that she is, she wrote back. A few Google searches later and the three of us had formed a 'mutual admiration society', by looking at each other's work online.

Rufus Wainwright, *Los Angeles Magazine*, the *New Yorker* and other press outlets around the world continue to shower Deven with praise ranging from 'Comedy Performer of the Decade' to 'Funniest Video of the Year'. Her most infamous and hysterical series, 'Welcome to my Home', parodies a former soap opera star's very 1980s-esque 'How To' series, complete with padded shoulders, beaded gowns, exer-cycles and enormous hair dos. More recently, Deven found new comedy mines to harvest and is lauded now for playing Betty Bowers: America's Best Christian and the elegantly filthy Talking Vajeene. Along with Joel, she travels the world entertaining audiences, ranging from drag queen bingo parlors to federal penitentiaries to armed forces battalions. This busy gal is also a professional ice skater and devoted collector of Pez dispensers!

Hunky Joel works constantly in the theater, TV and movie biz as well as on the stand-up stage, scoring supporting roles in everything from *Valkyrie* and *Heartbreak Kid* to *The Defenders* and *Criminal Minds*. With his knack for accents and dialects, he's also a sought-after voiceover artist and you've probably heard his talents in scads of television and radio commercials as well as in animated features and series.

We all decided to make a spoof video together, with me playing myself: the intrepid Entertainment reporter. Joel operated the camera. This is how we met! They arrived at my office on my lunch hour and it was love at first sight. We improvised a skit, Deven and Joel worked their editing magic and not only was a hilarious new video born, so was a brilliant new friendship! Hundreds of thousands of Deven's 'junkies' made it a highly rated—and still highly quotable—sensation!

Leggy, lithe Deven is often my date for red carpet events and parties (I'd take Joel, too, but I only get two tickets for these kinds of things and she just looks better in the gowns!) and the two of them have become part of my extended Hollywood family. New Year's Eve, Easter, Halloween, birthdays … Deven and Joel are always part of the celebration and never fail to make my home a haha hacienda!

Svelte Deven has a very healthy appetite, even if you can put your arms around her twice when giving her a hug! With beefy Joel at her side, they're certainly a dynamic duo.

Since Joel is such a he-man, I mentioned some of the stars I see at the gym, including Neil Patrick Harris. It turns out that Joel and Freddie Prinze Jr both went to high school with Neil in Albuquerque, New Mexico, back when he was famously starring as Doogie Howser, MD. I asked if everyone knew Neil was gay back then.

Joel: No! And I don't know if even he did! You'd see him with a girl, here or there. He'd come back from Hollywood for a semester at a time. I was the lead in the school play and he'd come back and end up doing lights for the show. And I remember thinking, 'I'm starring in a show and Doogie Howser's doing the tech work. Man, this is how it should be!' And then I wound up doing lights for a show he did … and then we did a show together at the end of the year.

Nelson: Did he go to the prom?

Joel: He did. With a girl. You didn't really hear rumors about him. He was Doogie … that's all we knew!

Nelson: So he escaped high school bullying because he was famous?

Joel: Oh, he'd get bullied. If we went out on a school trip, people would ask him for autographs. And if he didn't do it, people would start chanting 'Doogie sucks! Doogie sucks!'

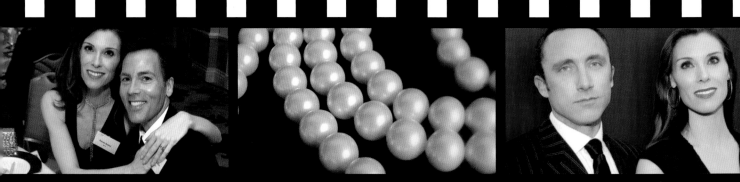

Deven has some amazing road stories about touring the world with their comedy act. Talk about a captive audience! 'When Joel and I were asked to perform in an all-male, maximum-security prison, we had the most dedicated audience ever. The convicts had all the time in the world to watch and laugh. I did ask the prisoners, "Do you watch *Prison Break*?" They said, "Yes!" That was their weekly brainstorming session!'

And proving that travel isn't as glamorous as it's cracked up to be, she recounts, 'We were in a rush to get to the airport to fly to a big show and Joel needed his pants hemmed. I am no seamstress so I stapled the hell out of his pants on the double inner seam—Joel had no clue. He never made it past airport security. The agent's wand kept going crazy at his pants. I had used so many staples they weren't going to let him on the flight. When Joel realized what I had done he was laughing so hard he had tears coming down his face trying to explain that I was the culprit.'

I believe if you're a funny person, funny things tend to happen to you. That's certainly the case with these two. 'Joel and I were hired to perform our comedy show for a private function at the Beverly Hills Hotel. While Joel was in the washroom I asked the concierge where the party was since I was the entertainment (I just assumed he'd know there was a comedy act booked). He looked me straight in the eye and asked, "When will the other girls arrive?" What a backhanded compliment! He thought I was a Beverly Hills hooker!'

If you're wondering how you can hire Deven and Joel to perform at your next function, here's their helpful guideline to remember: 'We have been offered to be paid in drugs, sex and weed instead of money. We always take the money.'

(L-R): Joel let me borrow Deven for a night on the town!
Joel and Deven. Photo by TheBuiBrothers.com

Celery (Celeriac) Remoulade

A staple of French cuisine, delicious Celery Remoulade is a favorite appetizer of mine and one of the very few dishes where I can tolerate the presence of mayonnaise. Celeriac (celery root) has become easy to find in the supermarkets, but don't let its homely appearance discourage you. Once you trim away its exterior, work quickly or it will discolor. It's great to make this a day or two in advance, because it actually softens and absorbs the flavors while in the refrigerator.

1½ teaspoon salt, plus an additional ¼ teaspoon salt

1 lemon, juiced

1 celery root, scrubbed and trimmed

¼ cup (2oz, 60gm) Dijon mustard

2 tablespoons olive oil

2 tablespoons white vinegar

3 tablespoons fresh parsley, chopped

$^1/_3$ cup (2½fl oz, 70ml) mayonnaise

- -

Combine 1½ teaspoons salt and the juice of one lemon in a large bowl.

Peel and quarter the trimmed celery root, then shred in food processor.
Combine with lemon juice and salt, tossing to coat well. Let sit for 15–20 minutes. The lemon juice will tenderize the celery root, and keep it from discoloring. Meanwhile, you can make the dressing.

In a bowl, whisk mustard and 2 tablespoons boiling water until combined.
Slowly drizzle olive oil into the mixture, continuing to whisk.
Drizzle in vinegar and salt, continuing to whisk.

Set aside dressing and rinse shredded celery in a strainer, squeezing out excess moisture.
Place in the large bowl and toss with dressing until well coated. Stir in parsley.
Gently fold in mayonnaise and store in the refrigerator until ready to serve.

Mini Caprese Appetizers

Rather than serve a traditional Caprese salad, why not pass around this bite-sized version before dinner to whet guests' appetites? Use 24 toothpicks for hors d'oeuvres, or 6 skewers to turn it into a proper plated course.

24 grape tomatoes
1½ cups (12oz, 350gm) mozzarella cheese, cubed
2 tablespoons olive oil
2 teaspoons balsamic vinegar
2 tablespoons fresh basil leaves, finely chopped
1 pinch kosher salt
1 pinch black pepper or red pepper flakes
24 toothpicks or 6 skewers

Toss tomatoes, cheese cubes, olive oil, vinegar, basil, salt and pepper together in a bowl until well coated.

Skewer one tomato and one piece of mozzarella cheese on each toothpick for hors d'ouevres, or 4 per skewer for a larger serve.

" Like the pizza Margarita, this dish was conceived as a tri-colored salute to the Italian flag: white, red and green. It's a much newer addition to the Italiano cucina, having originated in the 1950s from the Isle of Capri in the Campagna region. "

Chicken Parmesan

A crispy, healthier alternative to the Italian classic.

4 boneless, skinless chicken breasts
2 cups (16oz, 480gm) seasoned Italian breadcrumbs
4 tablespoons grated Parmesan cheese
4 egg whites
salt and black pepper to taste
1 tablespoon olive oil
2 garlic cloves, chopped
3 tablespoons unsalted butter
4 tablespoons capers
1 tablespoon Dijon mustard
juice of 2 lemons
4 tablespoons fresh Italian parsley, chopped

- -

Cover the chicken breasts in plastic wrap and pound them until they are ¼in (5mm) thick.

Combine crumbs and cheese in a large bowl. In another bowl, beat egg whites lightly.
Season breasts with salt and pepper to taste.
Dip each one into the egg whites and then the crumb mixture, until evenly coated.

In large pan, sauté oil and garlic over medium-high heat.
Add the breasts and cook until coating is deeply browned (approx 3–4 minutes).
Turn them over for 2–3 more minutes, then set aside on a platter.

While pan is still hot, reduce to medium heat and add butter.
As soon as it begins to brown, stir in capers, mustard and the juice of the lemons.
Remove from heat and add the parsley, mixing in the brown bits from the side of the pan.

Serve the breasts topped with the pan sauce. Delicious with a side of garlic steamed vegetables.

I'm told that chicken parmesan became a popular dish when people preferred to save money on the traditional version from 18th century Parma, Italy. That recipe called for veal, but poultry is less expensive.

Greek Orzo Chicken Bake

4 cups (8fl oz, 240ml) chicken broth
1 tablespoon butter
1¼ teaspoons kosher salt
¼ teaspoon black pepper
1 lb (450gm) chicken tenderloins, cut into 1in (2.5cm) pieces
1 lb (450gm) orzo (risoni)
2 cups (16oz, 480gm) crumbled feta cheese
¼ cup (2oz, 60gm) fresh dill, chopped
2 teaspoons lemon zest, grated
1 tablespoon fresh lemon juice
1 cup (8oz, 240gm) Parmesan, grated

Preheat oven to 400°F (200°C).

In a saucepan, bring broth, ¾ cup (6fl oz, 180ml) water, butter, salt and pepper to a boil.

In a baking dish, combine chicken, orzo, feta, dill, lemon zest and juice.
Pour broth mixture over orzo and stir just enough to mix.

Bake until orzo is tender and cooking liquid is creamy, approximately 40 minutes.
Sprinkle Parmesan on top and let stand for 5 minutes before serving.

Crabby Macaroni and Cheese

This is heavy fare, so I suggest it as a side dish—but it's certainly filling enough to stand on its own as a main course.

1 lb (450gm) elbow macaroni
4 cups (1 pint, 950ml) milk
8 tablespoons unsalted butter, divided
½ cup (4oz, 120gm) flour
¾ cup (7oz, 200gm) Gruyere cheese, grated
⅔ cup (5oz, 150gm) sharp Cheddar, grated
⅔ cup (5oz, 150gm) Parmesan, grated
½ teaspoon black pepper
1½ lb (700gm) lump crabmeat
1½ cups (12oz, 350gm) breadcrumbs
1 tablespoon salt

- -

Preheat oven to 375˚F (190˚C).

Place macaroni into a pot of boiling salted water. Cook until al dente, drain.

While the pasta cooks, warm the milk in a saucepan.
In another large pot over low heat, melt two-thirds of the butter and add flour.
Whisk until blended, then add the milk and continue cooking until smooth and thickened.

Remove from heat. Add the cheeses, salt and pepper.
Finally, add the pasta and crab, stirring well. Place the mixture in casserole dish or baking pan.

In the saucepan, melt the remaining butter and mix with the breadcrumbs. Sprinkle this mixture over the top of the casserole and bake until brown and bubbly (approximately 30 minutes).

Mint Nanaimo Bars

Deven brought me this recipe from her native Canada, where it is a very popular dessert. It's named for a coastal city in British Columbia and requires no baking ... but a lot of discipline to keep from overindulging once they're ready!

Bottom layer
½ cup (4oz, 120gm) unsalted butter
¼ cup (2oz, 60gm) granulated white sugar
$\frac{1}{3}$ cup (2½oz, 70gm) unsweetened cocoa
1 large egg, beaten
1 teaspoon pure vanilla extract
2 cups (16oz, 480gm) graham cracker crumbs (or any plain biscuit crumbs)
1 cup (8oz, 240gm) coconut
½ cup (4oz, 120gm) walnuts or pecans, coarsely chopped

Middle layer
¼ cup (2oz, 60gm) unsalted butter, room temperature
2–3 tablespoons milk or cream
2 tablespoons vanilla custard powder or vanilla pudding powder
½ teaspoon peppermint extract
2 cups (16oz, 480gm) powdered sugar (icing sugar)
drop of green food coloring (optional)

Top layer
8oz (1 cup, 240gm) bag of chocolate chips
1 tablespoon unsalted butter

Melt the butter in a saucepan.
Stir in the sugar and cocoa powder, and gradually whisk in the beaten egg.
Stir constantly until it thickens (1–2 minutes).

Remove from heat and stir in the vanilla extract, graham cracker crumbs, coconut and chopped nuts.

Press the mixture evenly onto the bottom of a non-stick pan, or one sprayed in cooking oil.
Cover and refrigerate until firm (about an hour).

Beat the butter with an electric mixer until smooth and creamy.
Add the remaining ingredients and beat until the mixture is smooth.

Spread the filling over the bottom layer then cover and refrigerate until firm (about 30 minutes).

Melt the chocolate and butter in a microwave or in a double boiler.
Spread the melted chocolate evenly over the filling and refrigerate until the chocolate has set.
Cut into squares.

Heather Pennell

Louise Pennell

Mark Pennell

Cameron Daddo

An Aussie Barbecue
with American Flavor

Dinner with

Cameron Daddo
Louise Pennell
Mark Pennell
Heather Pennell

Menu

Pork Loin with Honey Sauce
Asparagus with Honey Garlic Sauce
Dinner Rolls
Carrot Spice Cake

Suggested Wine

Monchhof Estate Riesling

Yes, the United States does have a 'National Honey Board,' which makes sense since they claim that the average American consumes 1.29 lb of the sweet stuff every year, made tastier by the fact that there are more than 300 different kinds available. If you're a fan, here's an entire menu from the Honey Board that puts nature's own sweetener to excellent use! The fact that the pork loin is grilled gives you a good excuse to invite some Australians (as I have!), who love commandeering the 'barbie!'

The guests at this dinner party are all natives of beautiful Melbourne, Australia: a city I visited all-too briefly. But as I arrived at my hotel, I was swept up in the crowds of runners in their annual Melbourne Marathon, so I felt right at home!

The Pennells have been close friends since my days working with journalist Louise Pennell. She and I clicked right away and have been great mates ever since. After she left her reporting job with the Seven Network, I introduced her to my terrific agent, and in no time at all she was dazzling viewers of the Fox Business Network. She's gone on to report for Bloomberg Television as well, and now heads up a dynamic media training industry with offices all over the world. Her brother, Mark, is a dashing theater and film producer. Their folks, Heather and John, are especially dear to me, and I consider them my own 'Aussie parents'.

Heather was an Australian variety TV and recording star in her youth and we've shared many musical theater moments over the years of our friendship: from being an appreciative audience for Hugh Jackman, Catherine Zeta Jones and Etta James, to singing onstage together in my cabaret show *Wake Up with Nelson!*, to singalong nights gathered around my piano at home and, memorably, a special performance at Louise's wedding. (Imagine my performance anxiety with her friends like Jodie Foster and Hugh Jackman on the guest list!) Heather and I are incorrigible as a duo—we don't need any excuse to break into song. Plus, she has the added benefit of knowing how to tap dance and soft shoe. (Don't let Louise, Mark or their brother John fool you, either ... they also know an impressive amount of fancy footwork, learned from their effervescent mum!) They're longtime family friends with Hugh and his wife, Deborra-Lee Furness, which was how I was initially introduced to them.

Of course, because the entertainment industry is a small one (especially in Melbourne), they also are longtime friends with suave, talented actor/ director Cameron Daddo. Most recognizable for his work on TV series like *F/X*, *Models Inc*, *Hope Island* and *24*, Cameron's one of Australia's well-known 'Daddo Brothers,' but certainly stands on his own in Hollywood as a sought-after leading man. I actually met him independently of the Pennells when he and I were invited to help promote the arrival of the famed racing trophy, the Melbourne Cup, in Hollywood. Like so many of his countrymen, he's a down-to-earth bloke with a great sense of humor and affable personality. He and his wife Alison Brahe are also devoted parents to their kids Lotus, Bodhi and River.

Nelson: Cameron, you had a nice career going in Oz. What made you decide to take the leap to Hollywood?

Cameron: In '92, things were cooking along quite nicely. I had married Alison, had just signed music recording and publishing deals and won a Logie Award for my acting in the mini-series Track of Glory. I had yet to crack the feature film medium... came very close, but no cigar. My agent had just returned from a trip to Hollywood and, unbeknownst to me, had quietly showed my demo reel around and received favorable responses. Back in Sydney, she pronounced in our living room that it was time for us to go to the US. Alison was horrified at the thought. I couldn't see anything but stars, stripes and the Hollywood sign! It was less than a year into our marriage... and we started over from scratch.

Nelson: How long before it paid off?

Cameron: It didn't take long before I landed my first job... a couple of months. A movie of the week, with my old Aussie friend Rod Hardy directing. Interesting, he was the first director I had ever worked with in Australia years before. I did have to take a few survival jobs, though ... telephone sales, landscaping, parking cars and a soy candle business!

Nelson: Is Australia such a 'small town' that all you famous Aussies know each other?

Mark: *That's true. But it's both a blessing and a curse. We have tremendous opportunities in Oz to hone our skills and jumpstart our careers, but it's a curse because to get professional opportunities and achieve bigger things, it's necessary we go offshore. That means those that travel abroad are all a part of the same alumni ... affectionately known as the 'Gum Nut Mafia.'*

Heather: *Back in the '50s, I appeared on John Conrad's teenage show with the Allen Brothers—one half of which was Peter Allen! One day, we'd had a few hiccoughs with the music and things weren't going right during rehearsals. The Allen Brothers were backing my performance and Peter was already writing words and music. When I made a comment about how it 'wasn't my night tonight,' Peter instantly composed music and lyrics from the phrase. 'It's Not My Night Tonight', wasn't a big hit, but I'll remember it forever! Years later, I had the pleasure of seeing Hugh play Peter in* The Boy From Oz, *on the opening night in New York City!*

Nelson: Mark, weren't you and Hugh's wife in each other's wedding parties? Explain that, please!

Mark: *Yes, I was Deborra-Lee's bridesman. I also laid out a breakfast in the Botanical Gardens in Melbourne to create a romantic environment for Hugh to propose to her.*

Nelson: So Hugh's always been down-to-earth?

Louise: *With Hugh, what you see is what you get. He has the same humble and caring approach with his friends now as he did when he was an unknown actor twenty years ago.*

Heather: *I agree. When we first met him, he had a little garden in his backyard that he tended to with great care. He's always been a terrific person.*

(L-R): Working on set with Louise. Bottom left: Broadway backstage, in Hugh's dressing room. Holding the Melbourne Cup with Cameron Daddo. Photo by Jeff Blaylock Rayner.

Mark: Australians by nature are egalitarian. Money, power or position does not make you a good bloke. Someone who will take the time with another person without looking down on him qualifies as a good bloke. That holds currency in Australia and I think that is what a lot of our actors take with them.

Nelson: Growing up, who were your showbiz idols?

Heather: Lana Turner for her glamour and acting skills. Doris Day for her versatility and vocal prowess. Clark Gable for his charisma. And Gene Kelly, whom I decided to marry when I was eight. If you've ever seen Anchors Aweigh, you'll know what I mean.

Louise: Grace Kelly ... I just wanted her life!

Heather: In my day, it was the big studios that created the business, which meant jobs for everyone. It also maintained that Hollywood glamour. Now I feel some of the polish has rubbed off and the glamour with it. We never heard negative stories about stars. It seemed to be a happier place.

Louise: I wish we had a little of that old Hollywood back. Frankly, I'm not that interested in Lindsay Lohan's drinking problems, but it seems to sell magazines.

Heather: Unfortunately, Australians have the 'tall poppy' culture: knocking those who have been successful. The funny thing is, in the end, Aussies are very proud of their exports.

Louise: Very true. Even though Kylie Minogue, Russell Crowe and Nicole Kidman routinely get knocked by the media, they're also revered for their success.

Nelson: Come on, Lou ... who's a tall poppy?

Louise: Well ... I do recall interviewing Sharon Stone. And being given only three minutes to do it! From the moment we sat down, she had it in her head that we'd met before. She embraced me like an old friend and asked how long it had been since we'd seen each other. I swear I had never met Sharon Stone in my life! When the camera started to roll and my three minutes suddenly became two minutes and fifty seconds, she continued to talk about how we must have met through some Australian contacts of hers. Despite my attempt to set her straight, she was convinced we knew each other. The time rolled down to two minutes and I still hadn't managed to force out my first question because she was still talking about how we'd met before. At the one minute and thirty second mark, the actress then talked about how wonderful I looked ... on and on she went about my outfit and how it made me look younger. Although I'm not really sure how she could tell, because we'd never met before! With just thirty seconds left, I was signaled to wrap up. That's when I realized she had managed to avoid giving me anything worthy to air on television. In a panic I tried to squeeze out just one question but it was too late, Ms Stone was out of her chair and ready for the next interview.

Nelson: Brendan Fraser did something very similar to me. Well, at least if she wanted to shut you down, she did it with a compliment!

Louise: Well, I must say ... I was slightly flattered.

Nelson: Cameron, you strike me as both a 'bloke' and a 'metrosexual'. You and Hugh have that in common. Any manscaping tips?

Cameron: Nothing in excess. I keep myself clean, simple and uncluttered. That goes for clothes, fragrance and style. Also a good pair of shoes, with the same color belt and a nice, simple watch ... you'll never go astray!

Good advice, whether you're going to a dinner party or a Hollywood casting call!

Pork Loin with Honey Sauce

1 cup (8oz, 240gm) chili
¾ cup (6fl oz, 180ml) honey
¼ cup (2oz, 60gm) onion, minced
2 tablespoons dry red wine
1 tablespoon Worcestershire sauce
1 teaspoon Dijon mustard
3 lb (1.5kg) lean pork loin

Combine all ingredients, except pork, in a large saucepan.
Bring to a boil over medium–high heat, stirring constantly. Remove from heat and keep warm.

Grill pork, covered, over medium–hot coals, turning and basting frequently with honey sauce, for about 1–1½ hours or until the meat thermometer registers 155–160°F (65–70°C).
Remove from grill, cover and keep warm for 15 minutes. Serve sliced with additional honey sauce.

Asparagus with Honey Garlic Sauce

2 lb (1kg) fresh asparagus
1 cup (8oz, 240gm) Dijon mustard
1 cup (8fl oz, 240ml) dark ale or dark beer
²/₃ cup (5fl oz, 140ml) honey
2 garlic cloves, minced
1 teaspoon dried thyme leaves, crushed
1 teaspoon salt

Add asparagus to boiling, salted water (about 1in (5mm)) and cook, covered, for about 2 minutes or until barely tender. Drain.

Combine mustard, ale, honey, garlic, thyme and salt; mix well. Pour over cooked asparagus.

" *Like onions and garlic, asparagus is a member of the lily family. Research indicates that it may help prevent and/or ease hangovers because it boosts levels of the key enzymes that break down alcohol in the liver.* "

Dinner Rolls

Growing up, my mother used to serve up dinner for seven nightly (I'm the youngest of five kids) and looking back, I don't know how she did it. She never seemed stressed out and always had time for us and managed to greet my Dad at the door with a martini in hand ... and looking as gorgeous as Betty Draper on Mad Men. *The one thing she was never able to accomplish, however, was getting the dinner rolls to the table without a fire extinguisher. It was always the one thing that slipped her mind and sometime in between finishing saying Grace and getting the first bite of food in our mouths, she would literally leap from her chair and dash back into the kitchen with a throaty, 'Jesus Christ ... the rolls!' She'd return a minute later, exasperated, with a cooking sheet full of smoking, black bricks. Hopefully, you'll remember to take these out of the oven in time. If not, do what my mother used to do: spread a little peanut butter on top and make them into doggie biscuits for the pooch!*

4 cups (2 pints, 950ml) milk
1 cup (8oz, 240gm) sugar
1 cup (8fl oz, 240ml) vegetable oil
9 cups (4½ lb, 2.1kg) flour
4½ teaspoons active dry yeast
1 teaspoon baking powder
1 teaspoon baking soda
2 tablespoons salt
Butter for muffin pans

- -

Preheat oven to 400°F (200°C).

Pour milk into a stockpot or Dutch oven. Add sugar and vegetable oil. Stir to combine.
Turn the burner to medium heat and heat the mixture until warm.

Add in 4 cups (2 lb, 950gm) flour and yeast. When yeast and flour are nicely
incorporated, add another 4 cups (2 lb, 950gm) of flour.
Stir together and allow to sit, covered with a towel or lid, for one hour.

After an hour, it will have doubled in size. Add 1 more cup (8oz, 240gm) of flour,
baking powder, baking soda and salt. Stir or knead lightly until combined.

Butter 1 or 2 muffin pans. Form the rolls by pinching off small pieces of
dough and rolling them into small balls. Place three balls of dough into each cup.
Cover and allow to rise for another 1–2 hours.

Bake until golden brown, about 20 minutes.

An Aussie Barbecue with American Flavor

Carrot Spice Cake

½ cup (4oz, 120gm) butter
1 cup (8fl oz, 240ml) honey
2 eggs
2 cups (16oz, 480gm) carrots, finely grated
½ cup (4oz, 120gm) golden raisins
½ cup (4oz, 120gm) chopped nuts
¼ cup (2fl oz, 60ml) orange juice
2 teaspoons vanilla

1 cup (8oz, 240gm) wholewheat flour
1 cup (8oz, 240gm) unbleached flour
2 teaspoons baking powder
1½ teaspoons ground cinnamon
1 teaspoon baking soda
½ teaspoon salt
½ teaspoon ground ginger
¼ tablespoon ground nutmeg

Preheat oven to 350°F (180°C).

In large mixing bowl, cream butter until fluffy.
Beat in honey in a fine stream until well blended.
Add eggs one at a time, beating well after each addition.

In small bowl, combine carrots, raisins, nuts, orange juice and vanilla. Set aside.

Add dry ingredients to creamed mixture alternately with carrot mixture, beginning and ending with dry ingredients. Turn batter into a greased 12 x 8 x 2in (30 x 20 x 5cm) pan.

Bake 35–45 minutes or until a wooden pick inserted near center comes out clean.
Cool in pan for 10 minutes, then turn onto wire cake rack.

The Greek soldiers who hid inside the legendary Trojan Horse were said to have consumed large quantities of raw carrots in order to inactivate their bowels. Strange ... I never thought of this delicious vegetable, so rich in vitamin A, to be binding! All things in moderation, I guess...

Dean Karnazes

Jared Crouch

Kathrine Switzer

Layne Beachley

An Athlete's Choice: Light and Healthy

Dinner with

Dean Karnazes
Kathrine Switzer
Jared Crouch
Layne Beachley

Menu

Simple Salmon Salad
Spinach Lasagna with a simple green
side salad and breadsticks
or
Eggplant Casserole
Roasted Root Vegetables with Sweet Balsamic Dressing
Jo's Strawberry Rhubarb Pie

Suggested Wine

Any of Crouchy's 'Brother's Parade' reds or
Kathrine's favorite Kiwi merlot, 'Harrier Rise'

One of the absolute best things about my life is the good fortune to meet so many public figures who inspire me, personally. This sometimes comes as a result of my television work—meeting icons of the show business world who occasionally manage to live up to their reputations. But as a 'weekend warrior' and late-in-life athlete, some of my idols come from the sports world. They inspire me to live and train for health and fitness, but having become friends with them, they also inspire me as kind-hearted, supportive human beings. It's my pleasure to introduce you to four tremendous sports figures, who are even more spectacular for the quality and content of their characters.

Dean Karnazes' running accomplishments are vast enough to fill volumes, but suffice to say the 'Ultramarathon Man' has parlayed his amazing, superhuman endurance prowess to become a pop culture phenomenon and even ranks as one of *Time* magazine's '100 Most Influential People'. In addition to all his accolades and accomplishments, he is a passionate advocate for children's fitness and one of the nicest guys I have the pleasure of knowing. We first met via email when I interviewed him for a magazine, but it was on the trails of the Catalina Eco-Marathon that we finally met in person and have been close mates and colleagues ever since.

Beautiful Kathrine Switzer made international headlines in 1967 when she became the first woman to run the previously men's only Boston Marathon, with a numbered entry (she registered as 'K V Switzer'). When the race director physically tried to drag her out of the event, she became a civil rights icon and has spent the last four decades living up to that responsibility. She is an outstanding ambassador, not only for women, but for anyone who enjoys the sport of marathoning. She even won the 1974 New York City Marathon and continues to race to this day. I met her while in Bermuda to run a marathon. We hit it off from the get-go and have remained friends ever since. Her excellent book, *Marathon Woman*, is one of my favorite autobiographies. I hope to visit her in New Zealand sometime soon and enjoy a run together in her adopted homeland.

Jared 'Crouchy' Crouch played for the Australian Football League's Sydney Swans, which is how I met him while filming a comedy segment on my first visit Down Under. He and his teammate, Leapin' Leo Barry, were such good sports that we bonded instantly. It didn't hurt that he has his own label of first-class wine from South Australia, 'Brothers Parade.' He and his stunning wife, Bec, have become close mates, and we make a point of spending time together when we're lucky enough to be in the same city.

At your next barbeque, try Crouchy's own personal marinade … if you can handle the yeasty Aussie secret ingredient, Vegemite! Yuck! I'm told it's an acquired taste, but not one I've been able to acquire!

¼ cup (2fl oz, 60ml) red wine
2 tablespoons tomato paste
1 tablespoon olive oil
1 tablespoon Vegemite
A few drops of Tabasco sauce

Combine all ingredients. Pour over meat of your choice and marinate overnight in fridge.

Vivacious Layne Beachley became a professional surfer as a teenager and ranked sixth in the world at age 20. Amazingly, she is the first woman to win seven World Championships. An icon of Australian sports, I first met her at a 'G'day LA' event in California to promote international tourism. She recognized me from my TV work, and the next thing I knew, we were hugging on the grass with someone in a giant koala costume sandwiched between us. It's been a love-fest ever since!

Q: What's a typical Layne Beachley dinner? 'My husband is the master chef. Traveling the world with INXS for the last 35 years has taught Kirk valuable kitchen skills, so I only have to cook when he doesn't feel like it. I'm allergic to yeast and wheat and lactose intolerant so my favorite meal to make is pizza. Yeast-free wheat crusts covered in tomato paste, chopped basil and garlic, topped with pumpkin, broccoli, snow peas, caramelized onion and goat feta. Yum!'

One of the strangest things for a career athlete to experience is having fame thrust upon him or her! And of course, they not only become celebrities as a result of their accomplishments; they get courted by other well-known folks who want to bask in their auras.

Dean says, 'I've met a number of stars and we've talked about going running together, but few have actually taken me up on it. Even if I promise it would only be a short run, I've still only had a few takers.' He laughs, 'I'd like to go running with Tom Hanks some day, since people always liken me to Forrest Gump.'

He appeared on David Letterman's late night talk show. I ask if that induced any stage fright. 'Letterman was really cool to me,' Dean explains. 'He's been a runner, so I think he could relate to some of my stories. We had fun together. But, yes … I was nervous as hell!'

I ask Kathrine when she first realized she was famous and she pinpointed the moment with her characteristic precision! 'It was about 1am, April 20, 1967. Twelve hours earlier I was running the Boston Marathon [April 19] when the race director attacked me at the two mile mark and tried to throw me out of the race, because I was a girl, and because I was wearing bib numbers in his race, which he felt was a men's only event, although this was not written anywhere in the entry requirements or in the rule book. My burly boyfriend, who was running alongside me, threw the official out instead and I went on to finish. My teammates and I thought this was just an oddball occurrence in what was a fairly weird event at the time anyway, but that all changed at 1am when we stopped on the thruway on the way home to Syracuse from Boston. We needed coffee, ice cream and a stretch and while we were in the diner, we saw the newspapers: front, back and center, the Boston Shoving Incident was everywhere … the incident had happened in front of the press truck! The photos were flashed around the world even before we finished. After that, it was *The Tonight Show*, global interviews … and thirteen years of hard running and legislation to prove I was right, and eventually getting the women's marathon into the Olympic Games!'

'Being famous wasn't something I ever thought of,' Jared admits. 'But I had to adapt when I "made it". Once you become public property, you have to live to the highest standards even if the same rules don't apply to the general public. You do get invited to some pretty cool parties, though!'

Layne was given the daunting task of giving teen heartthrob Zac Efron private surfing lessons when he visited Australia's Bondi Beach. 'I remember that mob scene as being anything but "private!"' Layne recalls. 'The best word to describe that experience is chaos! I don't think anyone was expecting the crowd to be as big or as excited as it turned out. The ear-piercing screams of the teenage girls, combined with the over-zealous paparazzi desperate to get near him gave me an insight into the crazy life this poor kid has to live. The random bloke who put his baby in Zac's lap as we were driving down the beach in the *Bondi Rescue* buggy was the craziest moment of all! I had to ask him what it was like to idolized and adored by girls yet to reach puberty and he replied, "It's kind of awkward."'

Had she an inkling that her love for sport would turn her into a notable public figure? Wide-eyed, she answers, 'Never in my wildest dreams! I entered into the world of surfing to become a world champion, so I'm very grateful for the opportunities it continues to create. It's rewarding to be known for achieving a goal, which also makes it easier to relate to other world champion athletes because we have a mutual understanding of self-sacrifice and dedication to our craft.'

Dean just laughs. 'The fact that I was positioned behind George Clooney and ahead of Oprah on *Time* magazine's 'Top 100 Most Influential People in the World' still boggles my mind. I think the voting was rigged!'

And the perks? Layne admits, 'People tend to go out of their way to help you. Plus, I'm constantly sent loads of wonderful products to try and get invited to great parties and functions such as lunch with Prince William, red carpet affairs with Clive Owen and after-parties with Michael Buble.'

Kathrine votes for the fact that, 'People answer your phone calls and emails. But there are as many downsides as perks. Biggest downside is that people ask for a lot of favors, and think you have time, money and paid assistants!'

'Hugh Jackman's at the top of my list of favorite celebrities I've met,' Jared tells me. 'I met him in LA when the Swans played an exhibition game there.

We had a great time chatting footy with his boy, Oscar. We also pushed Kylie Minogue around on a giant thong [flip-flop sandal] for the closing ceremonies at the Sydney Olympics. She was very nice as we spent a lot of time with her during the rehearsals.'

Jared tells the story of how Brother's Parade came to be. 'I grew up in Adelaide and my best mate, Trent Fraser, and I lived only two streets apart. He quickly became my fifth brother. The main road that connects our streets was called 'the Parade' and it would help shape our lives. As young boys we would ride our bikes up and down the Parade going to the local shops to get our sugar fix after school and kicking the football down at the local park. As we got older we both played junior football at the Norwood Football Club, the home ground of which is also called the Parade. It was here that my journey to become an AFL footballer began. I signed my first professional contract with the Sydney Swans in a hotel situated on the Parade. We had both just finished high school and Trent was working in the bottle shop at that same hotel. It was there that he first discovered a love for wine and went on to work at Penfolds winery … situated at the top of the Parade! I didn't start drinking until about the age of 24. All I wanted to be was a professional footballer and I couldn't see how alcohol was going to help me achieve this. Once I got to an age where I was able to understand and respect alcohol I learned that having a glass or two of wine wasn't going to hurt me. On a visit back to Adelaide, Trent introduced me to my first wine experience. The wine itself was a beautiful aged bottle of Yalumba Signature but what made it special was the environment. From that moment, our passion for wine developed and we eventually created Brothers Parade Wines: outstanding wines that are to be shared with your best mates. Just like Trent and I did all those years ago and continue to do today.'

(L-R): Celebrating Bermuda-style with Kathrine and my folks. Jared Crouch. Hosting a Q&A with dynamic Dean Karnazes. Laughing with Layne.

Simple Salmon Salad

Another easy-to-make-ahead dish. I don't like to go too heavy on the greens, preferring to make the salmon the star. In fact, I like to serve it on lettuce cups.

2 large salmon fillets (steamed or roasted)
2 stalks celery, diced
2 shallots (spring onions), diced
1 tablespoon capers
1 tablespoon fresh dill, finely chopped
1 tablespoon olive oil
1 tablespoon red wine vinegar
1 teaspoon fresh lemon juice
1 pinch kosher salt
¼ teaspoon black pepper
4–6 lettuce cups

Flake the chilled salmon into a bowl and add celery, onions, capers and dill. Toss.
Add oil, vinegar, lemon juice, salt and pepper and toss again. Scoop into lettuce cups and serve.

An Athlete's Choice: Light and Healthy

Spinach Lasagna

This is one of my favorite comfort foods—quick, easy and always a crowd-pleaser (and a good way to get the kids to eat their spinach!). Serve with a simple green side salad and a basket of crunchy breadsticks.

¼ cup (2oz, 60gm) butter
¼ cup (2oz, 60gm) all-purpose flour (plain flour)
1½ teaspoons salt
2½ cups (20fl oz, 600ml) milk
2 x 10oz (1¼ cups, 300gm) packages of frozen spinach, cooked and drained
½ teaspoon nutmeg
9 lasagna noodles (sheets), cooked
1 cup (8oz, 240gm) ricotta cheese or creamed cottage cheese
2 hard boiled eggs, sliced
Parmesan cheese, grated

Preheat oven to 375°F (190°C).

Over medium heat, melt butter in saucepan and stir in flour and salt until smooth. Gradually add milk. Stir until sauce just comes to a boil. Reduce heat to low and continue stirring constantly for 5 minutes. Combine 2 cups (16fl oz, 480ml) of the sauce with spinach and nutmeg, then set aside.

Pour half the remaining sauce into a greased baking dish and cover with 3 lasagna noodles. Spread half the spinach mixture over noodles. Divide half the ricotta and slices of 1 egg and layer on top. Repeat layering the noodles, spinach, cheese and egg. Top with remaining 3 noodles and pour the rest of the sauce over them. Sprinkle with Parmesan cheese and bake for 35 minutes, or until hot and bubbly. Let spinach lasagna stand for at least 10 minutes before serving.

The origin of lasagna is widely disputed. Most people assume it is an Italian dish, while British researchers say the dish dates back to the reign of Richard II in the 14th century. The word itself has Greek origins, leading some to believe that it was a method brought to the British Isles from the Roman Empire. Who cares where it comes from? It's delicious!

Eggplant Casserole

Outside of the US and Australia, 'eggplants' are often called 'aubergines'. No matter what you call them, they're delicious and nutritious and versatile for cooking! It is my understanding that smaller, immature eggplants are the best choices and, because they are extremely perishable, should be consumed within a day or two of purchase.

3 medium eggplants, peeled and sliced
½ cup (4oz, 120gm) butter
½ onion, finely chopped
Salt and pepper, to taste
3 eggs
1 cup (8fl oz, 240ml) milk
1 cup (8oz, 240gm) plain breadcrumbs
1 cup (8oz, 240gm) grated cheese (I prefer sharp cheddar)

Preheat oven to 350°F (180°C).

Cook peeled and sliced eggplant in boiling, salted water until soft. Drain and mash in large bowl.
Add butter, onion, salt, pepper and stir well.

In separate bowl, beat the eggs and add milk.

Add liquid to the eggplant. Add breadcrumbs and ½ cup (4oz, 120gm) grated cheese.
Bake in a casserole dish for 45 minutes.
Add remaining cheese on top and bake for another 2–3 minutes, until bubbling.

Roasted Root Vegetables with Sweet Balsamic Dressing

Ever since my former roommate, an English dynamo named Pam, introduced me to the magnificence of the parsnip, it has been one of my favorite vegetables! I consider it to be the lovechild of the potato and the carrot, so I love to make it for American friends whenever possible. Roasted veggies are a great side dish with almost any entree and I always make sure I prepare enough so that I can enjoy the leftovers, right from the fridge, the next day. Feel free to swap in other vegetables like red beets and celery root to suit your tastes.

5 large carrots, peeled, cut into ¾in (2cm) slices
1 large yam (sweet potato), peeled, cut into 1 x 1in (2.5cm) cubes
2 large potatoes, peeled, cut into 1 x 1in (2.5cm) cubes
2 turnips, peeled, cut into 1 x 1in (2.5cm) cubes
2 large parsnips, cut into ¾in (2cm) slices
1 large onion, peeled and quartered
3 yellow beets, peeled, cut into 1 x 1in (2.5cm) cubes
4 garlic cloves, peeled and halved
3 stalks celery, cut into ¾in (2cm) slices
1½ teaspoons garlic salt
2 sprigs fresh rosemary, chopped
Fresh ground black pepper, to taste

½ cup (4fl oz, 120ml) olive oil
¼ cup (2fl oz, 60ml) balsamic vinegar
⅓ cup (2½fl oz, 70ml) honey

Preheat oven to 375°F (190°C).

Toss dry ingredients in a deep baking dish. Add oil, vinegar and honey, and toss again.

Roast, uncovered, for approximately 30 minutes. Remove from oven and toss again.
Turn the heat up to 400°F (200°C) and return dish to oven. In 15–20 minutes, vegetables will caramelize.
Remove from oven and cover with foil until ready to serve.

Jo's Strawberry Rhubarb Pie

Now that my grandmother has gone to her greater reward in the sky, my friend Jo has the distinction of being the best baker I know. We met in 2003, working in the same office, and whenever a colleague had a birthday, she whipped up their favorite kind of cake as a treat for everyone. When July 1st rolled around, she asked me what I wanted so I replied 'a pie … a strawberry-rhubarb pie.' She came up with this delicious recipe and I have enjoyed it every year since!

Pastry for a 9in (23cm) two-crust pie
2 cups (16oz, 450gm) sugar, plus 1 teaspoon sugar
⅔ cup (5oz, 140gm) all-purpose flour (plain flour)
1 teaspoon grated orange peel
3 cups (6 stalks, 1½ lb, 700gm) rhubarb, chopped
3 cups (1½ lb, 700gm) strawberries, sliced in half
1 tablespoon butter

- -

Preheat oven to 425°F (225°C).

Prepare pastry.

Mix 2 cups (16oz, 480gm) sugar, flour and orange peel in large bowl. Stir in rhubarb and strawberries until well mixed. Turn into pastry-lined pie plate. Dot with butter. Cover with top crust that has slits cut into it. Seal and flute. Sprinkle with a teaspoon of sugar.

Bake for 55 minutes or until crust is brown and juice begins to bubble through slits in crust.

As tart and tasty as the rhubarb stalks are, discard the leaves if the grocer hasn't already. They're toxic!

An Athlete's Choice: Light and Healthy

Kathryn Joosten

James Arnold Taylor

Full of Character: Something Different

Dinner with

Kathryn Joosten
James Arnold Taylor

Menu

Shrimp Bisque
or
Crab Stuffed Mushrooms
Very Veggie Casserole
or
Irish Stew
Chocolate and Raspberry Cupcakes

Suggested Wine

Gangloff Condrieu (Dry White)

I f you ask most leading men and ladies what kind of roles they'd most like to play, it's almost always not the romantic hero or heroine. They'd prefer the juicier, more fun opportunities to play character parts. Those quirky, supporting figures are the backbone of any story and the actors cast as them are among Entertainment's most talented and respected … even if they don't always enjoy the name recognition of a Johnny Depp or Teri Hatcher.

I'm going to introduce you to two of the industry's most honored and in-demand character actors. One whose face you've surely seen a thousand times and one whose voice you've heard just as often!

Her comic timing and deadpan delivery has been heard in commercials, television and film. Kathryn Joosten won two Emmy Awards for her role as Karen McClusky on *Desperate Housewives*, and she showed off her dramatic chops memorably as the President's secretary, Dolores Landingham, in the long-running *The West Wing*. She began her career in middle age, proving that it's never too late to pursue one's dreams. She's also demonstrated resiliency by kicking lung cancer … twice! She's known around Hollywood not only as a gifted and reliable artist, but a generous and loyal friend.

Another always-busy working character actor is voice artist James Arnold Taylor. He's the official voice of animated superstars like Fred Flintstone, Teenage Mutant Ninja Turtle Leonardo, Obi-Wan Kenobi of *Star Wars: The Clone Wars* and scores of others. His spot-on mimicry and acting ability also make him the most sought-after 'voice double' for stars such as Christian Bale, Robin Williams, Ewan McGregor, Shia LaBeouf, Michael J Fox … the list goes on and on.

I first met Kathryn through her publicist, my college friend Thom DeLorenzo. Not surprisingly, it was on a red carpet! 'I am really uncomfortable on the red carpet,' she confides. 'I don't like posing for pictures. I like the interview possibilities, though, as I get to sound off on one thing or another and nowadays I get to use my celebrity status in my advocacy regarding lung cancer.' Another perk of fame, she admitted, is 'Not having to worry about where to park.' She still finds it a surprise when she's recognized. 'At the grocery store, I saw a gal I thought I recognized from home in Illinois and we kinda stared at each other. She also thought we'd met somewhere in

the past so we began the comparison of schools, towns, etc. But we then discovered it was actually from seeing each other on different TV shows! She was on *Big Love*.'

James has the opposite problem: not being recognized. But with his knack for imitation, he has a playful way of getting his revenge ... even if it is just coming out of the men's room. 'I held the door for Ron Howard and when he said, "Thank you", I answered him in his own voice and said, "You're welcome"!'

Playing second banana is something these pros got used to early ... and relish. 'Christopher Walken's reviews for a video game were glowing,' James told me. 'But it was my voice! And I voiced-over Christian Bale for a *Batman* trailer and that was the clip they played for him later to get him back into character. I guess I did my job right.'

When it comes to dinner parties, Kathryn and James have different ideas of what would be the ideal guest list. For Kathryn, her former co-star Martin Sheen would be her dream date. 'He's great fun and a terrific conversationalist. The relationship we showed on camera was about the same as it was off camera! He was the first big star I worked with and he made it so easy.' She wouldn't mind saving a place for Oscar winner, Tom Hanks, either. 'I think you can always tell when an actor is intelligent—when he's using his brain and not just his voice.'

Of course, when it comes to voices, no one can produce more than James. So his table would be surrounded by the likes of 'Daffy Duck, Porky Pig, Sylvester Junior and Boo Boo Bear. I like the sidekicks!'

You'd have to imagine that the Desperate Housewives would be experts at the whole dinner party thing. I had to ask Kathy which Housewife would throw the best dinner. Without hesitation, she said, 'Probably Bree. I think she [actress Marcia Cross] pretty much plays herself, as they all do. Except Teri is not a klutz and Marcia has a degree in child psychology.' I wonder which lady, among that vast ensemble, is she closest to? 'Probably Teri. We share being single parents. She very graciously contributed to a party I threw for the entire crew, and even arranged cupcakes and stayed for the party.' As for real-life dinner parties in Tinseltown, Kathryn quips, 'Every dinner

 Full of Character: Something Different

party in LA is a potential disaster because it's the custom here to blow off an invitation if you feel like it or get a better offer. One dinner I hosted went south when my guest arrived and announced she was not only a vegetarian, but a vegan. Try that one on for size at a moment's notice!' I've felt her pain before. That's why I always ask my guests about any dietary restrictions and keep a file. I have my designated Red Meat invitees and my Pasta Night pals!

Folks like these are really chameleons: you'll see them playing a politician one day and a homeless person the next. In James' case, he has to take on the vocal qualities of whatever A-lister he's dubbing. 'I've been Johnny Depp's official double, approved by him, starting back with Willy Wonka. Tim Burton was so secretive with *Alice in Wonderland* that he'd only give me 15 seconds of dialogue to practise matching him. And Johnny wanted my home phone number and my cell phone number so he could call and discuss the character with me if he needed. Much to my disappointment, he didn't call, but that meant that he approved of everything I did.' So he's gotten to be Willy Wonka, Captain Jack Sparrow and the Mad Hatter. The only other actor who can claim that is Depp himself!

I have to inquire if there is a voice he hasn't been able to master. 'Tobey Maguire! Our daughters are friends but I can't get his voice. Even though I did Spiderman's voice for some of the video games and have voiced other parts with Tobey, I just can't ever tune in to his voice. He's a really nice guy ... we're both vegans.' Uh oh, another vegan. I must make a notation in my files!

"

James' big break was doubling for Michael J Fox in Stuart Little. *'There was an open audition to voice match Michael, who was either not available or too expensive. Disney heard through the rumor mill that I was a spot-on match. Sometimes they'd cut me into the middle of a sentence of his and it had to be an exact match. Usually voices that are closest to my own are toughest. Shia LeBoeuf's is a little bit deeper than Michael's, but it's basically the same voice. If I do my job right, nobody knows I exist!'*

"

Shrimp Bisque

2 tablespoons butter
½ cup (4oz, 120gm) sweet onion, chopped
1 clove garlic, chopped
½ teaspoon paprika
1 teaspoon basil, chopped
1 cup (8 oz, 240gm) cream cheese, softened
1¼ cups (10 fl oz, 300ml) milk
2 x 10½oz (1¼ cups, 300 ml) cans condensed tomato soup
1 x 29oz (3½ cups, 800gm) can diced tomatoes with juice
1 lb (450gm) small cooked shrimp (prawns), peeled

Melt butter in a large saucepan. Add onion and sauté until softened. Add garlic and continue to sauté. Add paprika, basil, cream cheese and milk.

Stir over medium heat until smooth. Stir in canned soup and heat just to a boil. Add tomatoes with liquid and shrimp. Add as much water as necessary to achieve desired consistency and heat to serving temperature.

Garnish with chopped basil and whole shrimp, if desired.

Crab Stuffed Mushrooms

I was raised in mushroom country: Chester County, Pennsylvania, where mushroom houses abounded. Believe me, driving by, you always knew when to hold your nose! To this day, whenever someone tries to withhold information from me about a juicy story, I use the old Pennsylvanian adage, 'Stop treating me like a mushroom!' In other words, 'don't keep me in the dark and feed me a lot of manure!'

These appetizing appetizers are a breeze to make and just as easy to scarf down!

24 medium-sized mushrooms, washed and stemmed

1 x 6oz (180gm) can of crabmeat, rinsed and shredded

1 x 8oz (240gm) package of softened cream cheese

1 tablespoon whole milk

Fresh dill, finely chopped

Salt and pepper, to taste

- -

Preheat oven to 400°F (200°C).

Combine crabmeat and cream cheese in a bowl. Add milk. Add pepper, salt and dill to taste.
Stuff mushrooms with crab mixture. Bake for approximately 10 minutes and serve with toothpicks.

Very Veggie Casserole

This is a variation on the 'Tinseltown Tian' recipe from my last book, a staple of my diet because it's so filling, nutritious and adaptable to whatever produce tempts me at the Thursday Farmers Market in Century City! I make it as a main course for myself at least twice a week and, for parties, it is an easy side dish that will please everyone. You might even be able to sneak some Brussels sprouts in there past even the most finicky eater! By all means, change up the kinds of potato and cheese you use and experiment with various herbs. There are no rules here, just goodness!

1 large brown onion, sliced
Olive oil
Garlic salt and celery salt, to taste
Freshly ground pepper
2 large tomatoes, quartered
1 large (or 2 medium) Yukon Gold potatoes, peeled and sliced (not too thick)
1 large crown of broccoli, chopped into chunks
¼ cup (2oz, 60gm) grated cheese (gruyere is nice, so is cheddar)
Fresh herbs (basil or rosemary are my faves since I grow them in pots)

Preheat oven to 350°F (180°C).

Sauté sliced onion with olive oil over medium heat. Season liberally with celery salt and pepper. When translucent, transfer to a 2in (5cm) baking dish (sprayed with no-stick spray).

Arrange the sliced potatoes in a circle on top of the onion mixture. Add the remaining vegetables within the ring of potato slices in whatever design you prefer, keeping them tightly together, until all the onions are covered by the vegetables.

Drizzle olive oil over the top and add garlic salt and pepper to taste. Place fresh herbs on top of the dish and cover tightly with aluminum foil. Bake for 30 minutes.

Remove foil and herbs, add the grated cheese and place back in oven for another 30 minutes.

It will come out with the cheese brown and bubbling with the medley of steaming vegetables perfectly delicious, underneath! Oh my goodness, my mouth is watering!

Irish Stew

For six years and counting, I've had the pleasure of broadcasting to Ireland's well-loved afternoon TV lineup on RTE, The Afternoon Show. Since I just do the showbiz reports, I don't get to partake in the cooking segments, but it always seems to me that they have a passionate palate for simple fare and I'm invariably left with my mouth watering by the end of those demonstrations! Much to the dismay of many Europeans and Antipodeans, Americans don't eat a lot of lamb, so here's a recipe I use on St Patrick's Day to introduce my Yankee friends to the delicious, lean meat. Call me a lamb-bassador!

2 lb (1kg) boneless lamb shoulder, cut into 1in (2.5cm) cubes
4 medium potatoes, sliced ½ inch (1cm) thick
2 medium onions, sliced ¼ inch (5mm) thick
2 stalks celery, sliced ¼ inch (5mm) thick
4 medium carrots, peeled and sliced ¼ inch (5mm) thick
Salt and pepper to taste
2 tablespoons fresh thyme, coarsely chopped
2 tablespoons fresh parsley, coarsely chopped

- -

Preheat the oven to 325°F (160°C).

In a large casserole dish or Dutch oven, layer the ingredients in this sequence: lamb, potatoes, onions, celery and carrots. Sprinkle each layer with salt, pepper and thyme.

Add 1 cup (8fl oz, 240ml) water, cover, and slowly bring to a boil over medium-low heat.
Simmer for 5 minutes, then transfer the pot to the oven.
Keep covered and bake, without stirring, for 2–2½ hours or until the lamb is tender.

Sprinkle with chopped parsley and stir very gently to mix.

Chocolate and Raspberry Cupcakes

Ever since the ladies on Sex and the City *stopped by the Magnolia Bakery, cupcakes have been the trendy dessert of choice. It seems like every block in NYC these days has a cupcake shop. The muffin and bagel trends are a distant memory of the 20th century!*

Here's a tasty recipe that makes a decadent dessert your guests will enjoy—extra fancy when served on pretty plates with a scoop of high quality dark chocolate or vanilla ice cream (or fresh whipped cream if you prefer) and some extra raspberries.

¼ cup (2 oz, 60gm) bittersweet (dark) chocolate, coarsely chopped
2 eggs
1 cup (8oz, 240gm) brown sugar, firmly packed
½ cup (4oz, 120gm) butter, softened
⅔ cup (5 oz, 140gm) self-raising flour
2 tablespoons cocoa powder
⅓ cup (2½oz, 70gm) almond meal
½ cup (4oz, 120gm) frozen raspberries

Preheat oven to 335°F (165°C).

Line a 12-cupcake pan with cupcake papers.

Put the chocolate and ½ cup (4fl oz, 120ml) water into a saucepan over low heat, stir until smooth. Set aside.

Put eggs, sugar and butter in a large bowl. Beat with an electric mixer until combined.
Sift in flour and cocoa. Add the almond meal, stir to combine.

Stir in the warm chocolate mixture. Fold in the raspberries.

Divide mixture evenly into cake papers. Bake for 40–45 minutes until firm to touch.
Allow to cool a few minutes, then transfer to a wire rack.

Thom Racina

Kassie and James DePaiva

Marcia McCabe

Louan Gideon

Louise Shaffer

Philece Sampler

Soufflé with the Soap Stars

Dinner with

Kassie and James DePaiva
Thom Racina
Louan Gideon
Marcia McCabe
Philece Sampler
Louise Shaffer

Menu

Gruyere Soufflé
or
Baked Ziti with Ground Beef and Vegetables
Herb Roasted Potatoes
Dodgers Blueberry Bread Pudding
or
Lil's Cherry Cake

Suggested Wine

Prosecco Sparkling Wine

I grew up watching the 'soaps', thanks to my grandmother, and in my early career I enjoyed working in the genre as an actor, writer, casting assistant and production coordinator. By the time I hit Hollywood, I'd worked on *Search For Tomorrow*, *Loving*, *All My Children*, *Another World*, *As The World Turns*, *Guiding Light* and *One Life To Live*. My friend Marcia (who you'll meet in this chapter), says that being on a soap is like having a surrogate family, and I've always found that to be the case with the casts and crews on all these programs. Sadly, only two of those shows still exist, and the medium as a whole has so drastically changed as to be virtually unrecognizable to many of us 'old-timers'.

The professional skills I learned behind the scenes, from show running to storytelling, have been as invaluable to me as those I learned in front of the camera. Having logged thousands of hours in both live and taped TV, I still call on the tricks of the trade I learned from my mentor, daytime television legend Mary Stuart. Just as precious to me are the many friendships I made along the way. A quarter of a century later, many of my closest pals are from those happy days.

During this dinner party, I thought I'd introduce you to some of those well-known faces of classic American serial dramas who have enjoyed international fame because of their work in the exciting and glamorous make-believe world of soaps. There never would have been *Dynasty*, *Melrose Place* or *Gossip Girls* without them!

Southern belle Kassie DePaiva had a five-year stint as Chelsea Reardon on *Guiding Light*, but it is her nearly twenty-year run as the scheming Blair Cramer on *One Life to Live* for which she is best known. Through all the trials and tribulations her character has faced, it pales in comparison to the real life romance she shares with her former co-star, James, whom she married in 1996. They also have a son together.

James DePaiva is an actor I worked with back in the '80s at *One Life to Live*. He played the sly Max Holden for over a decade and gave me some of the best acting advice I ever received. When you get to the end of a scene and the camera lingers on you for dramatic effect, but you invariably have no bloody idea what the hell you're supposed to be playing, subtly pretend that

(L-R): With Marcia and Louan circa 1986 ... the era of Big Hair! Marcia always livened up even the most dramatic scenes! Trick or Treat with Philece.

Soufflé with the Soap Stars

you smell something bad. Really bad. That little squint of the eye and upturn of the nose can register as a variety of intense emotions. Go ahead, try it!

Soap scribe Thom Racina and I became buddies while I worked at *Another World*. He's an amazingly gifted storyteller and has authored several bestselling books. But daytime fans love him best for his outrageous 'Ice Princess' storyline on *General Hospital* that saw the entire city put into a scientific deep freeze! He also penned the love story of the genre's most iconic super couple, Luke and Laura. Hanging out with Thom is always a good time, especially when he tells true-life tales about his former personal assistant, Brad Pitt!

Louan Gideon and I became fast friends in the early '80s on the set of *One Life to Live* and wound up working together a few years later at *Search for Tomorrow* where she played Liza Sentell. (It was my great privilege to sneak her the storylines in advance when she came in to audition for the part. She nailed it!) You've probably seen her in many guest starring roles on shows like *Seinfeld*, *Malcolm In The Middle* and *The Secret World of Alex Mack*, but I know her for her wacky humor, spiritual strength and loyal kinship. She beat back breast cancer with more grace and panache than any of us could believe.

Also from *Search For Tomorrow* comes Marcia McCabe (investigative reporter Sunny Adamson for nearly a decade). Marcia was my very first friend when I worked on that show and she's been a surrogate sibling to me ever since. She's the biggest 'Cougar' in all of Manhattan ... as gorgeous as Grace Kelly and as fun as Ellen DeGeneres! She also had roles on *All My Children*, *One Life to Live*, *Another World* and *As the World Turns*.

Working in soaps, I made the greatest gal pals ... Philece Sampler certainly high ranking among them! We met when she was playing Donna Love on *Another World* (she'd just come from *Rituals* and *Days of Our Lives*), the mother of twin daughters—of course one was good and one was evil—both played by Anne Heche! Philece and I were practically living together by the time I moved to Los Angeles. We teamed for several offbeat writing jobs and were even Abyssinian cat breeders for a while!

Louise Shaffer and I met when she joined the cast of *Search for Tomorrow* as Stephanie Wyatt, fresh from her Emmy-winning turn as Rae Woodard on

(L-R): (Top) Go, Dodgers! Hugs in Hollywood! Thom Racina

Ryan's Hope. In addition to other stints on *All My Children* and *Guiding Light*, Louise has also written extensively for soaps and has authored five novels. She and her husband, Roger, are passionate animal lovers and have rescued dozens of animals over the years. She happens to be funny as hell, too!

Soap fans are notoriously passionate and it's not unheard of for them to occasionally mix-up actors with the characters they play. Thom tells me that during the zenith of *General Hospital*'s popularity, some actors who played bad guys had to have bodyguards to protect them from vengeful fans (let's not forget that 'fan' is short for 'fanatic!').

They also have long memories: a year after playing a young mother on *Search For Tomorrow*, Louise found herself on a bus sitting beside a viewer who was asking her what her character was up to 'these days' since leaving the mythical town of Henderson, USA. Trapped with nowhere to run, Louise decided to improvise. 'I told her that I was now in Spokane, Washington, and we spent the rest of the fifteen minute bus ride discussing my problem in adjusting my [fictional] child, Baby Libby, to her new home.' Hilarious and weird!

Philece was recognized by viewers of *Days of Our Lives*, who were so eagle-eyed that they identified her not so much by her appearance, but by her gestures! 'I was in a restaurant in Sacramento, California, and these two ladies politely introduced themselves and asked if I was Renee DiMera. When I said yes, they said, "I knew it! I could tell by the way you used your hands!" I never realized I used my hands so much when I was acting.'

Marcia shrugs. 'Most fans looked at me like a big sister and felt like they could confide in me. I was a ridiculously avid pen pal—and this was before email! A couple of the teenage girls I wrote to ended up becoming very good, lifelong friends.' She then remembers: 'There was one guy who wanted me to send him pictures of myself with my hair wrapped up in a white turban. That was weird! Needless to say, I didn't oblige him.'

Sometimes, it's just more frantic. Kassie had a fan that wanted a lock of her hair, which doesn't seem too out there (unless it's your hair they're after!) but her hubby Jim got tackled by an airport security guard, 'because she was so excited to see "Max!"'

Jim had his struggles on camera, too ... especially when Kassie's character was bed-hopping. 'It's not a pleasant thing, watching the one you love having a passionate love scene with someone else.' He does readily admit that 'meeting a great wife' was the biggest perk of the job, though. 'We met one night year before *One Life to Live*, when Kassie was singing at a club. But I completely forgot that night until we re-met on set and she reminded me.'

The medium is often a launching pad for young talent. Meg Ryan, Christopher Walken, Kylie Minogue, Susan Sarandon and Kevin Bacon are just some of the many stars who started out in soap operas. Did you know that Brad Pitt might never have wound up a movie star if he'd been more successful in soaps? He and Thom had quite a history, so I ask Thom to tell the tale.

'I needed a personal assistant and this cute kid showed up, full of energy and I hired him. It was Brad Pitt. He skimmed the pool, drove my scripts to the studio [this was before email], walked the dog. He moved in with me and we became very close. Good buddies. I came home from the studio early one day and I saw him doing an acting scene in my living room. I thought "this kid is very good". I told the producers at *Another World* about him and I wrote a two-year story for him. They brought him in for one day and the idiots, one after the other, said "He can't act", "He's not good looking", "He's got bad skin". Even the executive producer, John Whitesell, said to me "Thom I know he's your buddy, but I've gotta tell you ... this kid sucks. He'll never be an actor, tell him to go be a plumber." So I had to go home and tell Brad. And he cried, and I hugged him and said, "Now, listen, asshole! Go out and prove me right for believing in you!" And he did. But had they liked him [on the soap], he would have been [only] a soap star forever. God works in mysterious ways. But Brad did something for me, too. He told me I had to write a book and get out of soaps. So I wrote *Snow Angel*, which has a million copies in print, and that was all because of Brad. He pushed me to do that book and he gave me that renewed interest in writing novels.'

Gruyere Soufflé

1 dozen large eggs, separated
½ cup (4oz, 120gm) chives, chopped
2 teaspoons kosher salt
½ teaspoon black pepper
2 tablespoons unsalted butter
1 cup (8oz, 240gm) Gruyere cheese

- -

Preheat oven to 400°F (200°C).

In a large bowl, whisk together the egg yolks, chives, salt and pepper.
In a separate bowl, with an electric mixer on medium-high speed, beat the egg whites until stiff.
Using a spatula, gently fold egg whites into yolk mixture.

This is a large recipe, so use two nonstick skillets and make two
separate soufflés simultaneously on two burners.

Melt butter in skillets over medium-low heat. Add soufflé mixture and crumble the cheese over the top.
Bake until the eggs are puffy and golden, about 10 minutes. Cut into wedges to serve.

Baked Penne with Ground Beef & Vegetables

1 lb (450gm) ground (minced) hamburger
2 tablespoons olive oil
1 medium green pepper (capsicum)
1 medium red pepper (capsicum)
1 tablespoon garlic, minced
2 cups (16 oz, 480gm) canned tomatoes
½ cup (2fl oz, 60ml) dry red wine
1 cup (8fl oz, 240ml) canned tomato sauce
3 medium onions

1 tablespoon fresh basil, chopped
Salt and black pepper, to taste
¼ tablespoon dried oregano
½ cup (4oz, 120gm) ricotta cheese
¼ cup (2oz, 60gm) Parmesan cheese, grated
1 lb (450gm) fresh spinach
½ cup (4oz, 120gm) fresh mushrooms
1 cup (8oz, 240gm) ziti or penne
Non-stick cooking spray

Coarsely chop the onions, red and green peppers.
Wash, stem and chop the spinach and mushrooms. Meanwhile, cook the ziti and drain.
Because the pasta will be cooking additionally in the oven, it might be best to undercook it slightly.

Preheat oven to 375°F (190°C).

Heat 1 tablespoon of oil over medium heat and sauté the peppers for about 5 minutes.
Remove peppers with slotted spoon and set aside. Add remaining oil and sauté onions for about 3 minutes.
Add the hamburger (or sausage) and brown, breaking up the meat.
Add garlic and mushrooms and sauté for 2 more minutes. Drain excess fat.

Break up the tomatoes with a fork and add with the tomato sauce, wine, basil, salt, pepper and oregano.
Bring to a boil. Lower heat and cook, uncovered, for about 20 minutes.
Finally, add spinach and cook until wilted.

Coat a casserole dish with non-stick spray. Combine ziti, tomato mixture, ricotta and two thirds of the peppers in a large bowl, then spoon into casserole dish.
Sprinkle evenly with Parmesan. Bake for 25 minutes and garnish with rest of peppers.

Herb Roasted Potatoes

I could eat roasted potatoes like candy! (Frankly, I prefer savory over sweet in most things.) The crispier the better, in my opinion. So don't be afraid to let these babies continue to roast, to suit your taste!

4 pounds medium red potatoes, cut into 1in (2.5cm) pieces
8 sprigs fresh thyme
8 sprigs fresh rosemary
½ cup (4fl oz, 120ml) olive oil
garlic salt and black pepper to taste
juice of 1 large lemon

- -

Preheat oven to 400°F (200°C).

In a large roasting pan, toss the potatoes, thyme, rosemary, oil, salt and pepper to taste. Roast, stirring once halfway through, until golden brown and crisp, about 45–50 minutes.

Place in a large serving bowl and add the juice of 1 lemon, then toss and serve.

Dodgers Blue-Berry Bread Pudding

When it comes to athletics, I'm a late bloomer. As a kid, I had a congenital spine problem complicated by obesity that kept me from participating in gym class. Consequently, I kept getting bigger and bigger until I lost all the weight in my late teens through unhealthy fasting. I didn't discover exercise until my 20s, running until my mid-30s, and weight training and baseball until my 40s.

As for the baseball, I mean watching, not playing. After a particularly stressful day, I plopped down on the sofa with my dog, Lois, and channel surfed past a Los Angeles Dodgers game. Like many others who don't follow the sport, I had previously thought of it as a long affair played by paunchy, tobacco-spitting middle-aged men. For some reason, I was now rapt and relaxed at the same time. Watching the Dodgers alleviated my stress and completely captivated me.

I proudly wear my Dodgers blue jacket all season long—even, conspicuously, when I'm walking around in Manhattan: Yankees territory! And nothing's more fun than taking my international friends to Dodgers stadium for a game. Drinking beer, eating 'Dodger Dogs' and singing Take Me Out to the Ball Game at the 7th inning stretch are great traditions everyone can enjoy.

So in honor of the Los Angeles Dodgers, here's a Blue dessert just perfect for baseball season, or any time of year.

4 cups (2 lb, 950gm) bread, cut into small cubes
¼ cup (2oz, 60gm) butter, cut in pieces
⅔ cup (5oz, 140gm) sugar
¼ teaspoon salt
2 cups (16oz, 480gm) fresh or frozen blueberries
¼ cup (2fl oz, 60ml) water
2 tablespoons lemon juice
Heavy cream

- -

Preheat oven to 350°F (180°C).

In a large bowl, mix together all ingredients except the cream, then spread into a greased baking dish. Press ingredients down with the back of a wooden spoon. Bake until set, about 40 minutes.

When ready to serve, pour cream over the top. Blue and white—the Dodger's team colors!

"In 1883, the team originated in Brooklyn, New York. The nickname 'Dodgers' came from that of Brooklyn residents known as 'Trolley Dodgers' because of all the streetcars that traveled the streets at the time. They relocated to Los Angeles for the 1958 season and have been a fixture there ever since."

Lil's Coffee Cake

I don't remember who the heck Lil was, but I do remember my mother making this great cherry cake often. A great dessert to serve after you've left the dining room and moved into the den for coffee or liqueurs. Equally delish the next morning for breakfast (maybe you'll have overnight guests if the dinner party goes on too late)! Here's to you, Lil, whoever you were!

½ cup (4 oz, 120gm) butter
1 cup (8oz, 240gm) sugar
2 eggs
1 cup (8fl oz, 240ml) sour cream
1 teaspoon baking soda
2 cups (16oz, 480gm) flour
1 teaspoon baking powder
1 large jar of Maraschino cherries, drained and chopped

Preheat oven to 350°F (180°C).

Cream the butter and sugar and gradually mix in the eggs, sour cream and baking soda. Beat for 3 minutes at medium speed.

Sift together the flour and baking powder, then add to the mixture and beat for 2 minutes at medium speed.

Put half the batter into a cake pan and add the chopped cherries, spreading evenly. Then add the remaining half of the batter. Bake for 40 minutes.

Mindy Cohn

Alison Arngrim

Mimi Kennedy

A Chinese Banquet with Television Greats

Dinner with

Mindy Cohn
Mimi Kennedy
Alison Arngrim

Menu

Vegetarian Hot and Sour Soup
Chicken Fried Rice
Pepper Steak
or
Shrimp Stir Fry
Cold Sesame Noodles
Quick and Easy Almond Cookies

Suggested Wine

Hot or Cold Sake
(and Hot Green Tea, if you desire!)

This dinner party brings together three of classic TV's most popular character actresses. But, as you're about to discover over this Chinese food feast, there is much more to these great dames than just a trip down memory lane with *The Facts of Life*, *Dharma & Greg* and *Little House on the Prairie*.

Marvelous Mindy Cohn was discovered by producers of *The Facts of Life* while she was attending school in Los Angeles. Her long run as wisecracking brainiac Natalie (1979–1988 and the 2001 reunion movie) made her an indelible part of modern day pop culture. I first met her a decade or so ago, when I was teaching spin cardio classes. She's a surprisingly strong athlete and has that same winning smile and sense of humor we all knew so well from her onscreen work. For the last several years, she's also been the voice of Velma on the *Scooby Doo* cartoons, so listen closely next time you catch one of them!

Broadway and film star Mimi Kennedy is best known as the hippie mother of Jenna Elfman's character on the popular situation comedy *Dharma & Greg*. She and I had the same wonderful publicist for a while and I first met her when she came to be a guest speaker at my 'Brains and Brawn Workout' book club. (She penned a fascinating autobiography, *Taken to the Stage: The Education of an Actress*.) We also palled around at some fundraisers during the 2008 presidential campaigns. She's a brilliant, effervescent soul.

Hysterical Alison Arngrim will go down in TV history as one of the campiest characters ever to hit the small screen: nasty Nellie Oleson from the long

Alison and her childhood co-star Melissa Gilbert actually still reunite for dinner parties. She shares the fact that, 'I can always count on her to drop some fabulous bomb of what I call Historical Gossip: "Oh did I forget to tell you?" followed by some mind-blowing revelation about events in our shared childhoods. Thank God our husbands are there to keep order! It's always a toss up between Melissa and me as to who will cook—and no, unlike our characters, I don't lock her in the pantry and she doesn't put cayenne pepper in my food!'

A Chinese Banquet with Television Greats

running *Little House on the Prairie*. She celebrates the fame phenomenon but constantly proves she's the antithesis of that selfish, snotty little witch who tormented little Laura 'Half Pint' Ingalls (Melissa Gilbert). She's wildly funny on stage and off, and devotes a great deal of time to charitable causes, especially those related to child abuse and AIDS. One of my fondest memories is of having a tea party at her house, enjoying homemade scones, and getting a personal tour of her extensive memorabilia and snow-globe collections. (And yes, 'Nelson' and 'Nellie' did take turns trying on the infamous blonde curled wig … hysterical!)

After the tabloid feud frenzy between the actresses who played sisters Jan and Marcia on *The Brady Bunch*, how could I not ask about the current relationships with former co-stars? For Mindy, she says she's still friendly with all the girls. 'We are always aware of what's going on with each other and they are always in my heart. There's no dish, really. Even *E! Entertainment* couldn't come up with any smack on any of us!' But what about her most famous *Facts of Life* colleague—the young actor who played George grew up to be none other than George Clooney! Did she recognize his potential way back then? 'I don't think you can ever predict superstar status, but we all knew he was quite special, extremely talented and a very hard worker.'

Of course, George Clooney might be most women's dream dinner party date, but for Mimi it would be Oscar winner Benicio Del Toro. 'He would take me for tapas in Spain. And some sort of drink I've never had and a fabulous wine. We'd talk about the Spanish Civil War and Spanish art and how important it is to fight fascism. We wouldn't sleep together but we'd say we would if we weren't madly in love with our partners and we'd swear to remember this night the rest of our lives, even though we didn't sleep together.' Okay, okay, Mimi—we get it! You dig Benicio! (Although she cites her pals Danny DeVito and Rhea Perlman as the best real-life dinner party dates ''cause Danny knows good scotch and Rhea worries about her weight … which she doesn't need to do. So I could eat and drink fabulously and get tipsy but not too fat!')

Of course, even celebrities have dinner party disasters. Mimi's memorable mishap went something like this: 'The conversation at cocktails was about

sacrificial self-mutilation to atone for political crimes and one couple's big dog that enjoyed consuming his own ... well ... a conversation that should not precede a dinner party. Then the other husband insulted his wife. I think he called her an idiot. Then she called him something worse. There was a long pause. Somehow we got through it; my husband and I still wonder how. We still talk about it and it remains our worst experience hosting as a married couple. It was thirty years ago in our first apartment. They were fellow parents at our firstborn child's first school. We were trying to make a loving community of parents. That class, and the parents in it, remained fractious all the way through high school. We sighed with relief on graduation day!' Sounds like she learned her lesson about composing the proper guest list!

Alison has a memorable dinner debacle, too. 'Ahhh ... there was the time where one the guests drank himself into a stupor and strolled into the living room and took a nap in the middle of the floor. This might have gone totally unnoticed by the other guests who were all happily still chatting over dessert in the dining room, except for the fact that he then began to snore. Loudly. Really loudly. Like a buzz saw. He snored so loudly he frightened the cats. Everyone just stared at each other in horror. Finally one of the guests said conspiratorially, "Excuse me, but I think your cats want to know if anyone is going to do something about the grizzly bear in your living room." At that point everyone burst out laughing and so the evening was still remembered as a success. For them anyway. I don't know how things went later that night for Mr Grizzly, as the poor unfortunate Mrs Grizzly was not amused.'

(L-R) Multi-talented Mimi. Not-so-nasty Nellie: my pal Alison.

Vegetarian Hot and Sour Soup

Every morning when I broadcast via satellite to Australia, I hear the dulcet tones of my friend Heidi Peters, working in a dark little room called Master Control in the Sydney studios. I always look forward to seeing her whenever I'm in Sydney. After her holiday in the Orient, she sent me a thoughtful souvenir: an elegant set of chopsticks and holders for six. So, of course, I had to immediately brush up on my Chinese cooking skills!

This soup can be prepared ahead of time and frozen; just don't add the tofu or egg. When you're ready to serve, thaw the soup and add the tofu. When it comes to a boil, add the egg as directed below.

1 x 375g (12oz) cake fresh tofu
½ cup (4oz, 120gm) bamboo shoots
4 Chinese dried black mushrooms (or fresh mushrooms)
1 small handful dried lily buds
1 cup (8fl oz, 240ml) stock (chicken or vegetable)
1 teaspoon salt
1 teaspoon granulated sugar
2 tablespoons soy sauce
2½ tablespoons red rice or red wine vinegar
1 teaspoon sesame oil
1 tablespoon cornstarch (cornflour) dissolved in ¼ cup (2fl oz, 60ml) water
1 egg, beaten
1 green onion, finely chopped
black pepper to taste
hot chili oil, to taste (optional)

- -

Cut tofu into small squares. Cut bamboo shoots into thin strips, then into fine slices. To reconstitute the mushrooms, soak in warm water to soften, then cut off the stems and cut into thin strips. If using fresh mushrooms, wipe clean with a damp cloth and slice thinly.

To reconstitute lily buds, soak in hot water for 20 minutes to soften. Cut off any hard ends and cut buds in half.

Bring 6 cups (3 pints, 1.5 L) water and stock to a boil. When it is boiling, add the bamboo shoots, mushrooms and lily buds. Stir. Add the tofu. Bring back to a boil and stir in the salt, sugar, soy sauce, vinegar and sesame oil.

Mix cornstarch and water. Slowly pour the mixture into the soup, stirring as you add. Let the broth return to a boil, then remove from heat.

Slowly drop in the beaten egg and stir. Add the green onion and pepper to taste. Drizzle with chili oil if desired. Serve hot.

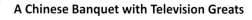

A Chinese Banquet with Television Greats

Chicken Fried Rice

2 eggs
2 tablespoons butter
2 tablespoons vegetable oil
2 medium brown onions, chopped
4 cups (2 lb, 950gm) cooked white rice, cold
4 tablespoons soy sauce
2 teaspoons black pepper
2 cups (16oz, 480gm) cooked, chopped chicken meat

In a small bowl, beat eggs with 2 tablespoons water. Melt butter in a large skillet over medium heat. Add eggs and leave unstirred for 2 minutes. Remove from skillet and shred eggs.

Heat oil in same skillet; add onion and sauté until soft. Then add rice, soy sauce, pepper and chicken. Stirfry together for 5 minutes, then stir in egg.

Pepper Steak

5 tablespoons cornstarch (cornflour)
2½ cups (20fl oz, 600ml) beef broth
2 tablespoons soy sauce
½ teaspoon garlic powder
1½ lb (750gm) boneless beef sirloin steak (approx ¾in (2cm))
3 cups (1½ lb, 750gm) fresh or frozen green or red pepper strips
1 large onion, sliced thinly
6 cups (3 lb, 1.5kg) hot cooked long-grain white rice
(Unless you prefer the Chicken Fried Rice as your only additional starch. I like to serve both.)

Mix cornstarch, broth, soy and garlic powder.
Slice beef into thin strips, then stirfry in nonstick skillet until browned.

Add peppers and onion. Add cornstarch mixture. Cook and stir until mixture boils and thickens.
Serve over white rice, or alongside the Chicken Fried Rice (following page).

Shrimp Stir Fry

⅓ cup (2½fl oz, 70ml) chicken broth
1 teaspoon rice wine vinegar
2 tablespoons soy sauce
½ teaspoon sesame oil
1 tablespoon sake
1 tablespoon cornstarch (cornflour)
1½ tablespoons vegetable oil
1½ teaspoons ginger, minced
4 cloves garlic, minced
3½ cups (29oz, 820gm) assorted fresh vegetables, chopped
8 red chilies, stemmed and left whole (optional)
1 lb (450gm) large shrimp (prawns), cleaned and deveined
Hot steamed rice, white or brown

- -

In a small bowl, mix together chicken broth, vinegar, soy sauce, sesame oil and sake. Set aside.
In another small bowl, stir together the cornstarch with 3 tablespoons water and set aside.

Heat oil over medium-high heat in a wok or large skillet; add ginger and garlic and sizzle briefly, then add
vegetables and chilies. Stir-fry for approximately 3 minutes, then add the shrimp.
Cook 2 more minutes or until shrimp turns pink. Add the sauce mixture and cook for another minute, then
stir in the cornstarch mixture until thickened (another minute). Serve over rice.

Cold Sesame Noodles

This mouth-watering dish makes a hearty appetizer or side dish, but you can also make it a main course for a picnic or al fresco dinner.

1 lb (450gm) udon noodles
6 green onions, cut into thin strips
2 celery stalks, cut into thin strips
2 carrots, cut into thin strips
⅓ cup (2½oz, 70gm) cilantro (coriander), chopped
4 tablespoons vegetable oil
2 tablespoons ginger, minced
6 garlic cloves, minced
⅓ cup (2½fl oz, 70ml) soy sauce
4 tablespoons vinegar
4 tablespoons sesame oil
4 teaspoons sugar
1 tablespoon sesame seeds

- -

Dip the udon noodles in boiling water for 30 seconds. Drain and rinse in cold water.
Place in a large bowl and mix in the onion, celery, carrot and cilantro.

Place vegetable oil in a pan over medium–high heat. Add ginger and garlic, sauté for 2 minutes.
Remove from heat and mix in soy sauce, vinegar, sesame oil and sugar.

Pour over the noodles and mix well.
Sprinkle sesame seeds over the top and refrigerate until ready to serve.

A Chinese Banquet with Television Greats

Quick and Easy Almond Cookies

What would a Chinese feast be without the almond cookies? Of course, if you prefer store-bought fortune cookies, that's easy. But these tasty treats can be made well in advance and are definitely more special. Whenever I order Chinese takeaway, I always save the fortunes and use them to decorate place settings, or tuck into greeting cards. Why not save some of your favorite fortunes to place on the side of the cookie plates?

2 cups (16oz, 480gm) all-purpose flour (plain flour)
½ teaspoon baking powder
½ teaspoon baking soda
⅛ teaspoon salt
½ cup (4oz, 120gm) butter
½ cup (4oz, 120gm) shortening
¾ cup (6oz, 180gm) white sugar
1 egg
2½ teaspoons almond extract
½ cup (4 oz, 120gm) whole, blanched almonds (one per cookie)
1 egg, lightly beaten

- -

Preheat oven to 325°F (160°C).

In a large bowl, sift flour, baking powder, baking soda and salt. In a medium bowl, use an electric mixer to beat the butter, shortening and sugar. Add the egg and almond extract and beat until well blended. Add to the flour mixture and mix well.

Use your fingers to form the crumbly mixture into dough and then form into two logs, 10–12in (25–30cm) long. Seal in plastic wrap and refrigerate for 2 hours.

Unwrap each log and lightly score the dough every ¾in (2cm) so you have 15 pieces. Cut the dough and roll each piece into a ball. Place on a lightly greased cookie tray, approximately 1½in (4cm) apart. Place an almond in the center of each cookie and press down lightly. Repeat with the remaining dough.

Brush each cookie lightly with beaten egg before baking. Bake for 15–18 minutes until golden brown. Cool and store in a sealed container.

Robert Nisbet

Bonnie Gillespie

El Coyote's Mexican Fiesta

Dinner with

Robert Nisbet
Bonnie Gillespie

Menu

Sweet and Savory Steak Salad
or
Roasted Veggie Salsa
El Coyote's Enchiladas Ranchera
Barb's Almond Toffee Ice Cream Log
or
Aunt Helen's Anise Cake

Suggested Beverage

Margaritas, of course! David O encourages you
to be daring and not settle only for traditional
tequila or beer accompaniments, but go out on a
liquor limb and try Brachuetto d'Acqui, a lightly
sparkling Italian red.

feel like I've known Robert and Bonnie forever! That just shows you how much I love them both …

Robert and I met when he first arrived in Los Angeles for one of his many radio and television reporting jobs for his native United Kingdom. We had worked together on the BBC's nightly entertainment show *Liquid News* but didn't meet in person until he was on the ground in Tinseltown. He's worn many hats for many outlets, but the siren call of showbiz news seems to constantly bring him back to sunny California (his new home base is in Washington, DC, where he covers the United States for *Sky News*). Ironically, our reunions often seem to be during tragic stories, such as covering the deaths of Heath Ledger, Michael Jackson or Farrah Fawcett. Running into mates and colleagues and sharing the history of times like those is a unique experience for journalists.

I met Bonnie when we both sat on a panel to advise aspiring actors. My specialty was on media training and publicity and she addressed them from the executive angle, as she is one of the busiest and most popular casting directors in town. She's the author of several books, including the best-selling *Self-Management for Actors: Getting Down to (Show) Business* and *Acting Qs: Conversations with Working Actors*. She's cast a wide range of famous names like Doris Roberts, Dan Castellaneta and Cybill Shepherd in addition to helping launch the careers of young talents like Scott Michael Foster and Alison Brie. She gives great advice and is always a heck of a lot of fun in the process. Together we founded the industry social networking group 'Hollywood Happy Hour', which continues to thrive under her expert guidance.

Bonnie describes the current state of Hollywood as 'the Wild West' but that it's a positive. 'It used to be somewhat linear for actors. You'd get to town, hustle to build up credits and training, sign with an agent and work your way up through one-line to co-star roles to (hopefully) starring roles in studio films. Now, the internet and the low cost of video equipment have leveled the playing field and actors who don't yet have representation are getting opportunities that were previously out of reach. They are creating their own content, building up a fan base and getting invited into rooms on major projects, bypassing much of the old way things were done.'

(L-R): Introducing friends to the wonders of El Coyote.
Robert Nisbet. My bonnie Bonnie.

We all agree that it pays to remain friendly from the beginning of your career—it will pay off handsomely when you're well known! Robert advises, 'Simply put: the nicest celebs are usually the ones who don't believe their own press releases. They're grounded enough to know they are just humans who have won life's lottery.'

Care to name some names, Robert?

'Ask any music journalist and I guarantee they will name Foo Fighters' Dave Grohl as the friendliest, most charming rock star in the mosh pit. He takes the time to ask you questions and even seems interested in the answers. I think being intelligent, thoughtful and plugged in to the world outside the movie set, recording studio or red carpet helps a star keep things in perspective.'

He continues, 'I spent several days in Africa with Bono as he campaigned for the world's richest countries to cancel the debt owed to them by the poorest. We traveled to some underprivileged areas of Ghana, but he never flagged, always signing autographs and playing with the children even when the cameras weren't rolling, which is often the real test! He often pulled up a chair with us at the end of the day and chatted knowledgeably and passionately about world affairs. A class act.'

You might think the most important qualities for an aspiring actor would be talent, looks, good fortune or 'connections.' But Bonnie thinks there's a different number one need for someone starting out in the 'biz. 'Stamina!' she exclaims. 'Yes, it's fabulous if you can also manage to be incredibly good-looking, amazingly talented, related to Spielberg, infinitely wealthy to invest in classes, publicists and your own projects, and super lucky. But really, without the stamina to stick it out, the ability to balance craft and business, and genuine love for the pursuit of it all, all those other things won't keep you successful for very long.'

And is there a time, if ever, that an actor should throw in the towel and call it quits?

'When it's no longer fun,' she states emphatically. 'No matter what line of work you're in—if you're miserable, you simply must choose another profession. Certainly, not every day is going to be a parade of awesome.

'The toughest part of getting to the top of the ladder, is getting through the crowd at the bottom.'

There will be hard times. It's a marathon, not a sprint, and it's important to build endurance and keep strong during the low times. You're going to be pursuing work much more of the time than you are actually working as an actor. If you can find ways to enjoy the pursuit, you're all set. If it's only the work that makes you happy, you may want to stay in a minor market (outside of a major city) and be a "big fish" there.'

Certainly Robert has been a 'big fish' in the news ocean for international reporting. That doesn't mean he hasn't had his share of foul-ups, mishaps and bloopers!

'I once had to cover a big celebration in Liverpool, the birthplace of the Beatles. The local soccer team had won a championship title and I was positioned outside the stadium's rowdiest pub to gauge the reaction. Hundreds of people had been availing themselves of the liquid refreshment for hours before I arrived. Every time the presenter crossed to me on live TV, the crowd dreamed up another humiliation. I had fright wigs put on my head, pints of beer poured over me and plenty of bare body parts revealed to the camera. But the piece de resistance was a mother who managed to drop a newborn baby into my arms just before I went live. I was so shocked—and the laughter was so loud—I just stared into the lens blankly.'

'Another time,' Robert remembers, 'I was recording a radio documentary about the life of extras in Hollywood, and was walking past a sound stage when I noticed my path was blocked by seven heavily sweating actors playing basketball. As I approached, one of them ran up to me and asked whether I would join their team to even up the numbers. It was George Clooney. Being English, and a little shy, I stammered, turned into a bumbling Hugh Grant and said I didn't know how to play and carried on walking, my eyes fixed on the ground. I told some friends about it afterward, who said the story would have been just a tad better if I'd actually taken him up on his offer.'

Sweet and Savory Steak Salad

I often make this for lunch, but it also works beautifully as a side salad as I'm using it on this menu. Of course you can make the steak at the same time, but something tells me if you're having a dinner party you are probably already busy enough! So why not make the steak the day before and thinly slice it to serve cold on top of this easy-to-prepare and delicious salad?

1 ripe pear
3 tablespoons olive oil
1 tablespoon fresh lemon juice
¼ teaspoon of salt
black pepper
1 x 10½oz (1¼ cups, 300gm) can Garbanzo beans (chickpeas), drained and rinsed
¾ cup (5 oz, 140gm) washed, mixed greens
½ cup (4 oz, 120gm) blue cheese, crumbled
1 lb (500gm) Sirloin steak, cooked and seasoned to taste, thinly sliced
rosemary sprigs or cilantro (coriander) stalks (optional)

Halve the pear and remove core. Then quarter and thickly slice.

Whisk olive oil slowly into the lemon juice, then whisk in salt and pepper.

Toss oil mixture and beans into greens, then top with crumbled cheese, pear slices and finally steak slices. Add rosemary or cilantro on top if desired.

Roasted Veggie Salsa

Living in California, I do get spoiled by all the excellent salsa available in our Mexican restaurants. There are also many good jarred brands on store shelves thanks to the worldwide popularity of that style of cuisine. While guacamole recipes are plentiful and easy (hello...? Avocado, lemon juice, Tabasco, a single diced tomato for color, salt and pepper is the greatest!), homemade salsa is often overlooked. Here's a version that's a little fancier for your next fiesta!

1¼ lb (560gm) plum tomatoes, halved

1 large red bell pepper (capsicum), stemmed and quartered lengthwise

1 medium onion, thinly sliced

4 cloves garlic

1 tablespoon olive oil

2 teaspoons lemon juice

¼ teaspoon red pepper flakes (or Tabasco sauce to taste)

Kosher salt, to taste

- -

Preheat broiler or grill.

Place tomatoes, pepper, onion and garlic with oil in a shallow baking pan and broil, turning occasionally, until lightly charred, about 10 minutes. Remove from broiler and let cool.

Peel garlic and puree in a blender with roasted vegetables, lemon juice, red pepper flakes and salt until it reaches the consistency you desire (I prefer chunky, but you may like it smooth).

El Coyote's Enchiladas Ranchera

My very favorite hangout in Los Angeles is the venerable El Coyote Café, established in 1931 and still family-owned. Their delicious, world-famous margaritas are like rocket fuel … and the festive atmosphere and friendly service always make for a memorable night out. It's forever packed with local Angelenos of every kind: families, oldsters, rockers, movie stars and romantic couples. I've celebrated more birthdays, anniversaries, first dates, break ups and make ups there than any other venue in the world! The owner, Margie, is the 'hostess with the most-est', and when you come in, tell Billy that I sent you!

Here is their renowned enchilada recipe. A fiesta for your tastebuds!

2 cloves garlic, finely chopped
2 onions, finely chopped (reserve some for enchilada sauce)
1 small can tomato puree
1 bell pepper, chopped
2 bay leaves
½ teaspoon oregano
1 x 26¼oz (750gm) can stewed tomatoes
¼ cup (2fl oz, 60ml) oil
12 flour tortillas
1 lb (450gm) sharp cheddar cheese, shredded
1 Ortega chili, thinly sliced
Sour cream (optional)

- -

Preheat oven to 350°F (180°C).

To make the Ranchera sauce, sauté garlic and one onion in a large saucepan.
Add tomato puree, pepper, bay leaves, oregano and stewed tomatoes. Season slightly with salt and pepper.
Cover and simmer for approximately 45 minutes.

Heat oil in a large skillet until very hot. Very quickly, dip tortillas in and out of the oil, then fill dipped tortillas with shredded cheese. Add some chopped onions, and roll tortillas.

Place rolled tortillas in 9 x 12in (23 x 30cm) baking pan. Top with Ranchera sauce and Ortega chili.

Bake until cheese is just melted. Serve sprinkled with more cheese and top with a dollop of sour cream, if desired.

Barb's Almond Toffee Ice Cream Log

My delightful friend, Barbara Northwood, is the Food Director for Australia's New Idea *magazine and a whiz in the kitchen. She makes terrific and tasty creations that are simple to prepare. The first time we ever made a meal together, a colorful Aussie lorikeet flew in the window! Since I didn't fancy a meal spoiled by parrot poop, I used a handy baguette to shoo it back out the window so Barb and I were able to resume our culinary pursuits. Shouldn't all kitchen windows be screened?*

Here's a recipe from Barbara's personal collection that she assures is not only quick and easy to make, but should be prepared in advance to save you extra time on the night of your dinner party.

Almond toffee:
1 cup (8oz, 240gm) blanched almonds, lightly toasted and cooled
1 cup (8oz, 240gm) sugar

8 cups (4 lb, 2kg) vanilla ice cream
2 teaspoons orange rind, finely grated
1 orange, segmented
1 mango, sliced
Fresh mint leaves, to decorate

Grease a large loaf pan. Line with plastic wrap, extending wrap over the sides.

To make almond toffee, sprinkle nuts over a greased oven tray. Place sugar and ½ cup (4fl oz, 120ml) water in a medium saucepan. Stir over a low heat until sugar is dissolved.
Bring to boil, without stirring, for about 5 minutes or until mixture turns golden brown and bubbles start to subside. Pour toffee over nuts. Stand at room temperature until set.
Break into large pieces and place pieces in a large snap-lock bag. Using a rolling pin, crush coarsely.

Place ice cream in a large bowl and allow to soften slightly. Beat with a wooden spoon until smooth.
Stir in rind and three-quarters of the crushed almond toffee. Pour into loaf pan.
Smooth over top. Freeze overnight.

When ready to serve, turn log out onto a large serving plate. Remove plastic wrap.
Top with orange segments and mango slices. Sprinkle with remaining almond toffee and decorate with mint.

Barb's tip: grate the rind from the orange before cutting into segments. To segment orange, cut peel and white pith from the orange using a sharp knife. Cut in between the membranes of the orange to remove segments. Do this over a bowl to catch the juice. The ice cream log can be made up to four days ahead. Keep covered, in freezer.

Aunt Helen's Anise Cake

My mom inherited Aunt Helen's recipe cards—all immaculately typed and individually sealed in plastic wrap, so you know they're tried and true favorites! 'Here's what's cookin' from the kitchen of Helen P. O'Sullivan!'

2 eggs
2 cups (16oz, 480gm) sugar
2½ cups (20oz, 600gm) flour
2½ teaspoons baking powder
1¼ cups (10fl oz, 300ml) milk
3 tablespoons anise seeds
½ cup (4oz, 140gm) margarine (melted)
1½ teaspoons lemon or orange extract

Preheat oven to 350°F (180°C).

Beat eggs and add sugar. Add dry ingredients alternately with milk.
Add anise seeds, melted margarine and citrus extract.

Bake in a greased tube pan for 45 minutes.

Aunt Helen's recipe card comments, 'This makes a good-sized cake and stays moist'.

James Denton

Erin Denton

A Desperate Housewives Dinner Party

Dinner with

James Denton
Erin Denton

Menu

Nutty Spinach Salad
or
Bacon-y Green Beans
Baked Salmon Dijon
or
Bean and Kale Pasta
Elegant Rosemary Cookies

Suggested Wine

An aged white Bordeaux

Over the years, I've done a thousand 'survival' jobs to make ends meet in between showbiz gigs; everything from script typist to bookstore clerk ... from spraying cologne in a department store to sketching caricatures at birthday parties. While I certainly prefer gigs that capitalize on my creative skills, all those jobs led to friendships and experiences I wouldn't have had otherwise, while providing a wage and reinforcing a work ethic.

Most of my non-TV positions were in the health and fitness industry, since I spent more than a decade as a certified trainer and aerobics instructor (as you may know, it was my being hired to instruct Princess Diana in that 'hot, new workout' of the late 1980s, 'step', that inadvertently led to my first regular position in morning television). Another performer who was making ends meet in the gym was my hard-bodied pal Erin O'Brien. While we were working at a health club in Los Angeles, she met and fell in love with actor James Denton. Some trainers have all the luck! Any of the romances I had with members always ended in dating disaster ... but for Erin and Jamie, it was the real deal and they've been happily married since 2002.

They're not only lucky at love, they have two great kids, Sheppard and Malin, and Erin wrote and starred in two successful workout programs, *Prenatal Fitness Fix* and *Postnatal Rescue*. Let me tell you, there's not an ounce of fat on her! And Jamie, of course, is known to millions of TV viewers for his role as Mike Delfino, the hunky plumber on the global phenomenon that is *Desperate Housewives*.

In spite of their showbiz success and performance prowess, the Dentons are the kind of friendly family you'd want as your own neighbors (away from the drama of Wisteria Lane). They are great fun to hang out with, especially

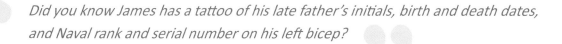

Did you know James has a tattoo of his late father's initials, birth and death dates, and Naval rank and serial number on his left bicep?

A Desperate Housewives Dinner Party

if Jamie's hosting a day out at the ballpark (he owns his own independent Minor League baseball team, the Fullerton Flyers) or jamming with his mates in their Band from TV, which also features Greg Grunberg from *Heroes* and Hugh Laurie from *House MD*; sometimes even Teri Hatcher drops in to sing a set with the boys as backup. We all got very involved in John Edwards' presidential campaign and it was a big disappointment for us when he lost out on the nomination ... but an even greater letdown when his secret, unscrupulous side came to light.

I was happy to catch up with the Dentons for a dinner party before they departed on their summer hiatus to Montana, where they annually escape the hoi polloi of Hollywood to enjoy some down-home family bonding time.

It might not surprise you to find out that James is great at the grill. As Erin says, 'He likes to light a cigar, open a cold, cheap domestic beer and chillax.' When the Denton clan entertains, that's usually where you can find him ... flipping meat on the barbeque while Erin whips up the sides. 'And he always helps with the dishes,' she is quick to point out. 'A true southern gentleman.'

They also believe that 'the key to entertaining a large group is: have fantastic cocktails!' But not everyone on the *Desperate Housewives* set is so casual with their hosting. 'We were just over at Teri Hatcher's for a dinner party and Wolfgang Puck prepared the meal!' Jamie tells me. 'It was the most extraordinary dining experience of my life. That woman knows how to throw a party!' (Having seen her in action, I suspect there was plenty of Chardonnay on hand!)

A remarkable aspect of a Denton family gathering is how well behaved the kids are—especially by Hollywood standards. When I was a child, we were practically held captive in our bedrooms until we learned how to mind our manners in the company of grown-ups, but that often seems to be a lost art in today's society. I always advise would-be dinner party hosts to do everyone a favor by hiring a pet-sitter and a baby-sitter when entertaining!

But Sheppard (8) and Malin (6) are good company. Is it the lack of sugar? (Erin admits 'I'm terrible at making desserts, so we never have them at home!') More likely it's skilful parenting. And it even translates when faced

> *Who would be the dream Denton dinner guests? With the exception of Erin, 'dreams' are all they could ever be!*
> *Jamie: 'Pistol' Pete Maravich (the late, legendary basketball star. He passed away at age 40, and his last words were reportedly, 'I feel great!')*
> *Erin: Dave Matthews. ('Then we'd have a hoot-a-nanny after dinner!')*
> *Sheppard: Michael Jackson!*
> *Malin: Sleeping Beauty!*

with the ultimate adults versus children challenge: dining out! 'Our kids are great in restaurants because we don't over estimate their abilities. We bring books, crayons and paper so they can doodle. We also order them a special dessert if we want to linger a bit longer over our dinner.'

The Dentons' ability to 'keep it real' amidst all the trappings that come with TV fame is why they're on my short list of favorite folks. Erin's always struck me as a grounded, no-nonsense gal and she made a wise choice in partners, because her husband is the same way. She explains, 'I think since Jamie's success came later in his career, he was an adult and able to handle it quite well. He also is quite aware that "fame" is fleeting, but being known as a quality human being is much more important. He's always tried to be very accommodating to fans—much to my annoyance, sometimes!' She gives me an example. 'There was only one time he wouldn't agree to getting his picture taken. We were home in Minnesota for Christmas at my Mom's church and after the service some kid walked up and said, "Mister, can I get my picture taken with you?" I looked at him and said, "Please don't," because we were with our family and it was really inappropriate. So Jamie said, "No, I'm sorry, I'm with my family ..." and when the kid's dad heard this, he looked at Jamie and said, "What a jerk!" So there you go ...'

Even with the nicest celebrities ... you win some, you lose some!

Nutty Spinach Salad

I love this tasty combination of flavors and textures. In addition to being easy to prepare, I think it's an excellent starter or side, especially with seafood dishes.

Honey Dijon Vinaigrette
2 tablespoons white wine vinegar
2 tablespoons honey
2 tablespoons Dijon mustard
1 garlic clove, minced
¼ teaspoon salt
¼ teaspoon black pepper
½ cup (4fl oz, 120ml) olive oil

1 cup (8 oz, 240gm) fresh baby spinach
½ cup (4 oz, 120gm) crumbled feta cheese
1 cup (8 oz, 240gm) dried cranberries
1 cup (8 oz, 240gm) walnut halves, toasted

In a small mixing bowl, whisk together vinegar, honey, mustard, garlic, salt and pepper. While continuing to whisk, slowly pour in oil until fully blended and slightly thickened.

In a large salad bowl, combine the spinach, feta cheese, cranberries and walnuts. Drizzle with vinaigrette; toss to coat. Serve immediately.

Bacon-y Green Beans

1 lb (450gm) green beans, trimmed
4 strips bacon
½ cup (4 oz, 120gm) blue cheese, crumbled
1½ cups (12oz, 350gm) toasted pecans, chopped
Salt and black pepper, to taste

Bring a large pot of salted water to a boil over high heat. Add the beans and blanch for only 2 minutes. Remove the beans from the water and immediately run under cold water. Set aside.

In a large skillet over medium heat, cook bacon until crisp. Set aside on paper towels.

Add the beans to the bacon grease and cook for another 2–3 minutes. Add cheese and stir until it just begins melting. Crumble the bacon into bits and add to mixture. Finally, stir in pecans and season with salt and pepper. Serve hot.

Baked Salmon Dijon

1 cup (8fl oz, 240ml) fat-free sour cream
2 tablespoons fresh dill, chopped
3 tablespoons shallots (spring onions), chopped
2 tablespoons Dijon mustard
2 tablespoons lemon juice
6 1/2 lb (3kg) salmon fillets with skin on, cut in center
Garlic salt and black pepper, to taste
Non-stick cooking spray

Preheat oven to 400°F (200°C).

Whisk sour cream, dill, scallions, mustard and lemon juice in a bowl.

Place salmon fillets (skin side down) on baking sheet.
Sprinkle with garlic salt and pepper, then spread on sauce mixture.

Bake salmon for 20–25 minutes.

A Desperate Housewives Dinner Party

Bean and Kale Pasta with Sun Dried Tomatoes and Bacon

There is a lot going on in this recipe, but I love all these tastes and textures together. It's a marvelous, unusual blend of sweet and smoky—a nice change from all the traditional tomato and cheese sauces that usually smother good pasta. You may use any pasta you like, but I find that a simple penne or fusilli suits this recipe best.

4 slices of bacon
1 onion, chopped
1 bunch of kale, thoroughly washed and torn into large pieces
3 garlic cloves, minced
1½ cups (12oz, 350gm) pasta
1 x 14½oz (400gm) can of white beans, drained and rinsed
1 cup (8oz, 240gm) sun dried tomatoes, coarsely chopped
1½ cups (12fl oz, 350ml) of stock (chicken broth or vegetable)
Kosher salt and pepper
Parmesan cheese, shaved

- -

Cook the bacon in a large saucepan over medium heat.
When it is cooked, remove and place it to the side, saving several tablespoons of fat in the pan.
Meanwhile, start a pot of salted water on another burner so it will be boiling for your pasta.

Add onions to the pan and cook on low heat until translucent. Increase heat to medium and add the kale, stirring occasionally. After kale wilts, add the garlic and cook for another minute.

When water is boiling, add pasta and cook, stirring occasionally.

Add beans and tomatoes to the saucepan, then the stock. Bring to a low simmer for ten minutes, stirring occasionally to gently blend and adding salt and pepper to taste. The kale will soften nicely.

Pour the drained pasta into a large bowl, saving a few ladles of the starchy pasta water to thicken the sauce, if needed. Pour sauce on top and gently mix.
Crumble bacon over the top and lightly shave some Parmesan cheese as a final touch.

Elegant Rosemary Cookies

½ cup (4 oz, 120gm) butter, softened
¾ cup (6 oz, 180gm) white sugar
1 medium egg
1 cup (8 oz, 240gm) wholewheat (wholemeal) flour
¾ cup (6 oz, 180gm) all-purpose flour (plain flour)
1 tablespoon finely chopped fresh rosemary
½ teaspoon baking powder

- -

Beat the butter and sugar together in a bowl until creamy and smooth,
and stir in the egg until well incorporated.
Stir in the wholewheat flour, all-purpose flour, rosemary, and baking powder until well blended.
Cut the dough into 2 equal-sized pieces, and shape each piece into a log about 1¼in (3cm) in diameter.
Wrap the logs in plastic wrap and refrigerate for at least 2 hours, or place in a freezer for about 1 hour.

Preheat oven to 350°F (180°F).

Line baking sheets with parchment paper.

Cut the logs of dough into thin slices, ⅛ to ¼in (2.5 to 3mm) thick. Place the slices on the prepared baking
sheets, and bake until the cookies are set and the edges turn golden brown, 10 to 12 minutes.
Cool for 1 minute on baking sheets before removing to wire racks to finish cooling.

Carolyn Seymour
Ian Abercrombie

New York, New York!

Dinner with

Ian Abercrombie
Carolyn Seymour

Menu
A Feast from Telepan, NYC!

Cosmo and Champers Cocktails
Lobster Bolognese
Asparagus with Roasted Shallots and Mustard Seeds
Chickpea Pancakes with Spicy Carrots and Oregano Oil
Lemon Verbena Crepes with Strawberries
or
Christopher's Authentic New York Cheesecake

Suggested Wine

Champagne!

Two of the UK's most talented ex-pats are friends and neighbors of mine in Hollywood, Ian Abercrombie and Carolyn Seymour. We've spent holidays together, as well as many dinner parties, and they even popped up to guest star in a performance of my live cabaret show *Wake Up with Nelson!* (It was at one of Carolyn's Christmas dinners that I first met Irmalin DiCaprio ... you never know what delightful person will turn up on her eclectic guest lists!) Their combined careers could fill an encyclopedia with theater, film and television credits and, while you may not recognize their names, you have certainly seen or heard them in action!

Ian has spent over four decades in show business racking up an impressive resume, co-starring alongside the likes of greats such as Jason Robards, Anthony Hopkins and Olivia DeHavilland, but it is his brilliant, comedic portrayal of Elaine's befuddled boss Mr Pitt on *Seinfeld* for which most people instantly recognize him. He has nothing but high praise for his comic foil, Julia Louis Dreyfus, but more interesting are all his tales of treading the boards in works as diverse as Ibsen and Lerner & Lowe. He even managed to find time to play the legendary character of Batman's butler Alfred Pennyworth in the *Birds of Prey* TV series. A new generation recognizes his distinctive voice as Chancellor Palpatine in the animated *Star Wars: The Clone Wars*.

Beautiful, classically trained Carolyn was a major star of the British West End theater world when she landed the leading role of Abby Grant in the cult favorite, post-apocalyptic 1970s BBC series *Survivors*. Hollywood soon beckoned and she continues to be a sought-after guest star in episodic television and, as is always the case with rabid sci-fi fans, she is a fan favorite at conventions for her roles in *Star Trek: Voyager*, *Quantum Leap* and *Star Trek: The Next Generation*. She continues to grace theater audiences with occasional stage appearances and also lends her dulcet tones to several animated series and video games.

The fact that these two are great chums always makes for an especially fun evening of chat and laughter.

Now ... let's talk about this particularly special menu!

One of the nicest things about living in Manhattan is the accessibility to some of the world's finest restaurants. Especially in my neighborhood, the

Upper West Side, great eateries of every imaginable cuisine can be found on every block. Among the best is Telepan, which is a short walk from my front door and boasts an elegant atmosphere, extensive wine list and amazing menu. For me, every trip to NYC includes a stop in for a visit, and it should for you, too! Reviewers have gushed about the 'clarity and focus of his food ... elegant and without gimmickry' and how the fare '... puts its faith in fundamental virtues; its freshness, the pureness or punch of the flavors; the skill with which it's been cooked.'

Recently, I was at the bar with my pal Marcia—she was sipping Prosecco and I was enjoying a Chardonnay—and she introduced me to the owner and chef, Bill Telepan. He opened his establishment in 2005, after training and working as an executive chef at several renowned restaurants like Le Bernardin, Gotham Bar and Grill and Ansonia. We hit it off instantly, because he is also a runner. He was rehabbing an injury and I turned him on to a line of awesome pool-running shoes. He was very appreciative, so I told him he could repay me by contributing a dinner party menu of items from his personal files. Here they are for you to enjoy!

With so many notables coming through his doors regularly, I assumed Bill was like most New Yorkers when it comes to encountering stars: low-key. He admitted that the only people he gets nervous cooking for are other chefs—makes sense. That said, he did tell me he'd love to host Radiohead, Bruce Springsteen and Angelina Jolie. If any of those folks invite you out for a meal in the Big Apple, definitely suggest making reservations at Telepan and give Bill a thrill!

... And be sure to say Nelson sent you.

Nelson: How has it all changed since you started in the business?

Ian: In the 1960s, Hollywood was fun and "hard work" was the key. One was treated with respect, no matter what your position. Good manners were a given. Encouragement was given openly. If you had talent it was recognized. We did not have to go through a myriad of people to book a job. Producers trusted casting directors and in turn, casting agents listened to the actors' agents when submitting a client. Many, many changes since then. Many, many not good.

Carolyn: It was a much more personal business predicated on talent. Now it's much more of a business on every level. You are a business and you have to market it as such. In the old days, the agents actually used to go out to studios and sell their clients. It's much tougher now. And they pay less than they ever used to!

Nelson: What would you advise young people who dream of "making it" in Hollywood?

Ian: First, don't cop an attitude, be gracious to everyone (you don't know who they may be!) ... get into a play to be seen ... and be clean (meaning hygiene).

Carolyn: Do everything and anything, I say. It opens you up to the experience of the business. Go to the theater, learn Shakespeare, learn about movement, breathing and voice. People have no voice anymore. Your voice is a muscle. It's all training, like at the gym. Then you'll have enormous range and you can convey all the emotion you want with just a sigh. It's all at your fingertips!

Ian: And keep dreaming! But make sure your goals are realistic. Be prepared for rejection—it's part of the process. Be determined, tenacious and if your passion is well placed, you are on your way. Above all, do not let your ego rule your decisions.

(L-R) Ian Abercrombie. Where I hang my hat in the Big Apple. Carolyn is simply ... divine! Check out that bone structure!

Cosmo and Champers Cocktails

Unlike most folks, I'm not big on champagne. I'd usually rather stick with white wine, but here's a fun champagne cocktail recipe I found online when planning a festive summer dinner party. It's very sweet and packs a little punch, pardon the pun. Of course, Sex and The City fans will like anything reminiscent of the Cosmopolitans that Carrie and her girlfriends used to swill!

1¼ cups (10fl oz, 300ml) Cointreau liqueur or Grand Marnier
1¼ cups (10fl oz, 300ml) cranberry juice
10 tablespoons fresh lime juice
3 tablespoons fine sugar
4 cups (2 pints, 950ml) chilled champagne

- -

Stir together Cointreau, juices, and sugar. Chill, covered, for at least 2 hours.
Just before serving, divide among flute glasses and top off with Champagne.

Lobster Bolognese

2 x 1¼-1 ½ lb (600–700gm) lobsters
1 cup (8fl oz, 240ml) chicken stock or water
⅛ cup (1oz, 30ml) white wine vinegar
Sea salt, to taste
1 shallot, minced
2 cloves garlic, minced

¼ cup (2fl oz, 60ml) extra virgin olive oil
1 x 14oz (400gm) can tomatoes, squeezed dry and chopped very fine
½ cup (4fl oz, 120ml) white wine
¾ cup (6fl oz, 180ml) white lobster or chicken stock

2 tablespoons butter
1 cup (8 oz, 240gm) spaghetti
2 tablespoons minced herbs (preferably tarragon, chervil, parsley, dill and/or chives)

- -

Ask your butcher to break apart the lobster into head, claws and tail.

Separate the tail and claws from the head and set aside.

Open up the head by pulling down the bottom leg half away from the top.
Scrape away and discard the feathery lungs and insides from the head.
Using a chef's knife, chop head into small pieces.

Place the heads in a pot with the stock. Bring to a simmer and cook for 15 minutes.
Set aside for 15 minutes, then strain and reserve.

Bring a pot of water to a rolling boil. Add enough vinegar to flavor the water and salt to taste like the sea.
Let water return to a rolling boil and add lobster tail and claws.
Reduce heat to medium and cook, uncovered. Watch carefully—do not let the water come to a boil again.
The pot should bubble occasionally but not simmer. Cook lobster tail for 5 minutes and claws for 7 minutes.
Remove from liquid and cool. Shell the tail, knuckles, and claws.

Sweat shallots and garlic in extra virgin olive oil until soft, about 7–8 minutes.
Add tomatoes and cook for about 5 minutes. Add wine and reduce until almost dry, about 3–5 minutes.
Add stock, bring to a simmer and cook for 5 minutes.

Bring lightly salted water to a boil, add spaghetti and cook for 7–8 minutes. Drain and add to sauce with
butter and cook until butter is incorporated into sauce.
Finally, add lobster meat and warm on medium heat, sprinkling with herbs.

Asparagus with Roasted Shallots and Mustard Seeds

6 tablespoons extra virgin olive oil
2 large shallots, peeled and sliced into 4 thick slices
Salt, to taste
1 tablespoon black mustard seeds
1 cup (8 oz, 240gm) asparagus, peeled if thick, cut into 2in (5cm) pieces
2 tablespoons vegetable stock or water

- -

Preheat oven to 400°F (200°C).

Place 1 tablespoon olive oil in a small ovenproof sauté pan. Put shallots in the pan and sprinkle with salt.
Turn stove on high and cook until shallots begin to sizzle.
Cover with a lid or foil and place in oven until tender but not falling apart, about 10–15 minutes.
Remove from oven and cool.

Make vinaigrette by placing juice, vinegar, mustard and a pinch of salt in a mixing bowl.
Whisk, slowly drizzling in 4 tablespoons of olive oil as you go. Check seasoning and reserve.

Heat a medium sauté pan on high and add remaining oil. When oil is just below smoking point, add
asparagus and cook until lightly brown, about 3–5 minutes depending on thickness.
Add shallots and toss for 30 seconds. Take off the flame, add seeds and toast for about 20–30 seconds.
Then add stock or water to prevent further browning.

Chickpea Pancakes with Spicy Carrots and Oregano Oil

Chickpea pancake
⅔ cup (5fl oz, 140ml) milk
1 tablespoon cream
1 egg
½ cup (4 oz, 120gm) flour
¼ cup (2oz, 60gm) chickpea flour
⅛ to ¼ teaspoon sugar
¼ teaspoon salt
½ teaspoon baking powder
¾ cup (6oz, 180gm) crushed cooked chickpeas
½ teaspoon butter

Pepperoncini mix
1 cup (8oz, 240gm) sliced onion
6 cloves garlic, thinly sliced
½ cup (4fl oz, 120ml) extra virgin olive oil
Salt, to taste
1 cup (8oz, 240gm) celery, peeled and cut on the bias
8 oven-roasted tomatoes, julienned
8 pepperoncini peppers, seeds removed from 2, julienned

Carrots
¼ cup (2oz, 60gm) butter
11/2 lb (700gm) multi-colored carrots, peeled
½ cup (4fl oz, 120ml) vegetable stock

Oregano oil
1 tablespoon chopped oregano
1 teaspoon red wine vinegar
2 tablespoons extra virgin olive oil

Preheat oven to 450°F (230°C).

Mix milk, cream and egg in a bowl. Add flours, sugar, salt and baking powder.
Fold crushed chickpeas into the batter. Melt butter in a medium ovenproof non-stick pan over high heat.
Swirl butter around pan. Use 2 tablespoons of batter to form a pancake 3in (7.5cm) in diameter.
Cook two at a time. When the edges start to lightly brown, about 1 to 2 minutes, place in the oven for 2 minutes. Flip the pancakes and return to oven until lightly brown, about 4 minutes.
Repeat with remaining batter. Keep pancakes warm.

Over medium–low heat, cook onion and garlic in olive oil with a pinch of salt in covered pan for 3 minutes. Add celery and another small pinch of salt and cook, covered, for another 5 minutes.
Add tomato and soften for 2 minutes. Add peppers and cook 3–4 minutes. Take off heat and allow to cool.
Cut the carrots into oblique 1in (2.5cm) segments by cutting on the bias and then rotating carrot 180 degrees before cutting again. Melt the butter in a large sauté pan over medium heat.
Add carrots, season with salt, and sweat for 6 minutes. Add stock and cook, uncovered, over medium-high heat until carrots are al dente and liquid forms a glaze, about 7 minutes. Mix together and set aside until use.

Place carrots and pepperoncini mix into a large sauté pan over medium-high heat. When warmed through, adjust seasoning. Serve on pancakes and drizzle with oregano oil.

Lemon Verbena Crepes with Strawberries

Crepe batter
2 eggs
¼ cup (2fl oz, 60ml) milk
½ cup (4fl oz, 120ml) seltzer, club soda (soda water)
1 tablespoon sugar
2 tablespoons melted butter
¼ teaspoon salt
½ cup (4oz, 120gm) all-purpose flour (plain flour)

Filling
½ cup (4fl oz, 120ml) milk
1 tablespoon dried verbena
1 tablespoon plus 1 teaspoon granulated sugar
1 egg yolk
1 egg
1 tablespoon cornstarch (cornflour)
2 tablespoons unsalted butter

Strawberries
⅓ cup (2½oz, 70gm) sugar
Juice of 2 lemons
3 tablespoons unsalted butter
1 lb (450gm) strawberries, cut into quarters

- -

Lightly beat the eggs in a medium-sized mixing bowl. Whisk in the milk, seltzer, sugar, melted butter and salt. Add the flour and whisk until lump-free and of pourable consistency.

Set a dinner plate next to the stove. Heat a 12in (30cm) sauté pan over low flame. Coat the pan with a thin layer of batter, (maximum ¼ cup (2fl oz, 60ml) per crepe), shaking and tilting the pan as you pour. Try to achieve an even layer. As soon as the crepe is solid and smells buttery, lift one edge with a spatula or your fingers and remove it to the dinner plate. Aim for blond, uncolored crepes. The batter is enough for 8 crepes, so you may choose the best looking and thinnest for the dessert ("best looking and thinnest?" How Hollywood!). Continue cooking the crepes, layering them on top of each other. Wrap and set aside.

Place the milk and verbena in a heavy-bottomed medium saucepan. Bring the milk to a boil and remove from heat. Add the granulated sugar and stir to dissolve. Steep for half an hour to infuse the milk with the verbena. In a mixing bowl, whisk the yolks and cornstarch into a smooth paste. Add a large ladleful of milk to the yolk mixture, whisk until smooth. Pour the yolk mixture into the remaining milk, whisking continuously. Over medium heat, stirring constantly, bring the filling to a boil. If the mixture begins to lump, immediately remove from the heat and whisk vigorously until smooth. Lower the heat and continue cooking to a boil. Once the filling has boiled, immediately pour into a bowl to cool. Blend in the butter, and place the bowl over an ice bath. Stir occasionally until room temperature. Refrigerate.

In a sauté pan, combine the sugar and lemon juice. Bring to a rolling boil, and add the butter. Add the strawberries to the pan and toss to coat. Cook until the berries are just warm through and juicy.

Spread ½ tablespoon of the filling on each crepe, and fold into quarters. Warm in a 350°F (180°C) oven.

Christopher's Authentic New York Cheesecake

Veteran New York-based actor/artist Christopher Durham gave me this foolproof recipe. He claims it was slipped to him by a pastry chef at one of his favorite Manhattan restaurants and that it's the most delicious of any 'authentic' New York cheesecake he's ever tasted … and easy to replicate in your own kitchen. Why not try putting him to the test? (Incidentally, I put him to the test by having him whip one up for me as a birthday present…and he passed with flying colors. It's great!)

1 lb (450gm) Ricotta cheese

1 lb (450ml) sour cream

1 lb (450gm) cream cheese

1½ cups (12oz, 350gm) sugar

½ cup (4oz, 120gm) butter, melted

3 large eggs

3 tablespoons flour

3 tablespoons cornstarch (cornflour)

4½ teaspoons vanilla extract

4½ teaspoons fresh lemon juice

Preheat oven to 350°F (180°C).

Place all ingredients in a large mixing bowl.

Begin beating with an electric mixer. Start on low, move to medium and finish on high speed for 10 minutes.

Batter will be smooth and liquid. Grease and lightly flour a round spring form bake pan 10in (25cm) in diameter. Pour batter into pan and bake for 1 hour. After 1 hour, turn the oven off and leave the cheesecake in the oven for an additional hour, then remove and refrigerate. Enjoy alone or with fresh berries on top.

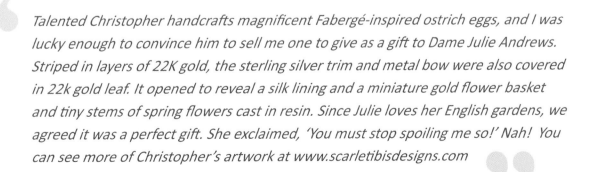

Talented Christopher handcrafts magnificent Fabergé-inspired ostrich eggs, and I was lucky enough to convince him to sell me one to give as a gift to Dame Julie Andrews. Striped in layers of 22K gold, the sterling silver trim and metal bow were also covered in 22k gold leaf. It opened to reveal a silk lining and a miniature gold flower basket and tiny stems of spring flowers cast in resin. Since Julie loves her English gardens, we agreed it was a perfect gift. She exclaimed, 'You must stop spoiling me so!' Nah! You can see more of Christopher's artwork at www.scarletibisdesigns.com

Jeffrey Werber

Gloria Allred

Limoncello with a Legal Lady and Lassie's Vet

Dinner with

Jeffrey Werber
Gloria Allred

Menu
Amy Casale's Specialties!

Veal Ossobucco
or
My Favourite Meatloaf
Creamy Polenta with Shiitake
Mushrooms and Manchego Cheese
Lemon Pecan Biscotti
Limoncello

Suggested Wine

Nero D'Avola (a bold Sicilian red)

For nearly two decades, the Emmy-winning 'Vet to the Stars', Jeffrey Werber, has also been the veterinarian to my beloved pets: the Abyssinian Henry and my springer spaniel Lois. He has most certainly been a part of their longevity, good health and happiness ... and his bedside manner has not only gone a long way with my four-legged friends, but he's always had a calming and reassuring affect on those of us who cherish them! He's a 24/7 kind of Doctor Doolittle and always seems to go above and beyond, not only for his A-list Hollywood celebrity clientele, but for the rest of us, too! And how cool is this? He is the official veterinarian for the most beloved collie in show business: Lassie!

Just as Jeff is at the top of his profession in veterinary medicine, so is my longtime buddy, attorney Gloria Allred, among the most distinguished (and often controversial!) in her field. This feminine-but-ferocious legal eagle is known for taking on the biggest names in the entertainment industry: from Michael Jackson and Tiger Woods to Aaron Spelling and OJ Simpson. She never backs down from a fight and is known and respected in showbiz circles as the champion of the underdog. I always tell her I sleep better at night knowing I have her on speed dial ... and that is true! She's as savvy in the courtroom as she is engaging before the TV cameras, but you might not suspect how warm and funny she is when she takes one of her all-too-brief breaks from work.

Gloria came to Los Angeles in 1966 as a single mother and worked as an inner-city high school English teacher before becoming one of the most famous attorneys in America. Raised to be an independent, self sufficient 'equal' in a distinctly 'man's world,' she reveals that her greatest influences were President John F Kennedy, because of the way his message of service to a higher cause resonated with her, and Lucy Ricardo from *I Love Lucy*, 'because she never stopped trying to step out from her husband's shadow'. If you've ever seen Glo at a press conference or in a courtroom, you know how fearless she is.

'How could I not be?' she asks, shrugging off how impressed I was by her tenacity. 'When I see injustice against women and minorities and how they've been treated in an unfair or harmful manner, I want to right the wrongs, to

(L-R): Jeff Werber, vet extraordinaire! With my beloved Lois. The late, great Abyssinian Henry. Gloria Allred, Wonder Woman!

 Limoncello with a Legal Lady and Lassie's Vet

If you're thinking of getting your pet into show business, Jeff has some words of advice: 'It all depends on the nature and personality of the animal. Dogs love to work. Many of them think they were placed here on this earth for one thing only: to please their masters. Even dogs that aren't will still perform and behave if you train them with positive reinforcement. But that doesn't apply to wild animals.'

When I mention how Steve Irwin and Siegfried and Roy had their love of wildlife backfire on them, he points out: 'The key word is wild. They cannot be domesticated. Roy would be the first one to tell you that the cat who attacked him was not there to hurt him. I would not trust a chimpanzee as far as I could throw one. They're adorable, but you can't kid yourself into thinking they can be pets. A lion cub can be cute and sociable, but it's not a pet. Leave them in the wild where they belong.'

vindicate and protect their rights in a court of law or in any manner that is possible. I want to empower them and improve their status and condition and make the public policy of our country that "equal opportunity" are not just words on a piece of paper, but a reality. I'm inspired by Gandhi who said, "You must be the change you wish to see in the world".'

Jeff continues to find inspiration in his patients: animals of all breeds, shapes and sizes. It's been his lifelong dedication that turned into a fulfilling career. I don't know if I'd call him a 'dog whisperer,' but he definitely has a special rapport with members of the animal kingdom. He believes that pets are the great equalizer for their human mascots, which is why his celebrity clientele rarely seem to cop attitude when they come in to his practice. 'I've found over the years that pets really bring everybody down to a level playing field. Many of my employees comment about the celebrities who come in and don't have airs about them—even if paparazzi are outside chasing behind them. They're normal and attentive to their pets. The most they might ask for is a house call, but generally they're wonderful … as is the experience of treating their pets. You see their tender sides. Kobe Bryant, even after he moved out of town, would come back to me, sending his Pomeranians to me in a limousine!'

Having the responsibility of being Lassie's personal vet is 'nothing special, really,' he admits. Did you know that all the Lassies have been male, even though in the scripts the dog is referred to as 'she?' (I suppose if he lifts his leg during a scene, that shot gets edited out!) Jeff does reveal the little known fact that all the Lassies are related. 'Lassie number nine is almost ten years old, so it only makes sense to have a Lassie number ten. Traditionally, they've all been sons of the prior Lassie, so the bloodline goes all the way back. They want the next generation to have the look and the elegance of the prior Lassie.'

Both my friends' sought-after expertise and commentary have made them popular TV personalities, but it's all thanks to their love and dedication to their respective professions. As for being a celebrity, Gloria reveals it isn't a state of being that occurs to her. 'Frankly, I don't even think about it. I'm thinking about the issues, being a strong advocate for my clients and working to win, waging the battle. That's what I'm thinking about every day.'

In charge of the menu for this dinner party extravaganza is another gifted person I'm honored to introduce.

One of the first friends I made when I moved to New York City was the very funny Amy Casale. She and I ended up in an acting class together and we hit it off instantly, launching a kinship that has spanned nearly three decades! We were definitely wild children in those early years and didn't slow down much when we relocated to Hollywood in our thirties. Now that we're in our forties, we've only managed to slow down a wee bit … probably more because we're so busy.

Amy followed in the footsteps of her talented mother, Anne, who authored severall bestselling cookbooks. Of course, everything Amy dishes up is served with a tremendous side of laughter—she's one of the funniest people I know! You must read her weekly blog on www.stillababe.com for great mealtime ideas and plenty of chuckles.

She was sweet enough to share some of her yummiest creations for our culinary delight. As she is fond of saying, 'Eating should always be a party in your mouth!' So enjoy …

Veal Ossobucco

4 large slices of veal shanks, about 2in (5cm) thick (your butcher will have sliced pieces available)
3 tablespoons unsalted butter
3 tablespoons olive oil
¼ cup (2oz, 60gm) flour
1 teaspoon fresh ground pepper
½ teaspoon kosher salt
1 medium sweet onion, chopped

3 carrots, peeled and chopped
2 sticks of celery, peeled and chopped
2 cloves of garlic, minced
1 tablespoon grated lemon rind (the rind of approximately 1 lemon)
1 cup (8fl oz, 240ml) dry vermouth
1 x 14.5 oz (400gm) can of petit diced tomatoes with juice

1 cup (8fl oz, 240ml) beef broth
1 bay leaf
2 teaspoons fresh minced thyme or 1 teaspoon dried thyme
2 tablespoons fresh chopped basil
¼ cup (2oz, 60gm) Italian parsley, chopped

Preheat oven to 350°F (180°C).

Tie the shanks with kitchen twine like a package: across the top and around the side.

In a large Dutch oven, (or another deep pot with a heavy lid), heat butter and olive oil over medium heat.

Combine flour, salt and pepper on a large plate and dredge veal shanks in the mix. Immediately place the shanks in the pan and sauté on all sides until golden brown. (You may have to do this in two batches to let the meat brown nicely.) Remove the shanks and set aside.

Add onion, carrots and celery. Stir often until golden, scraping the bottom of the pan to incorporate any fragments from the veal, about 7–10 minutes.

Add garlic, lemon rind and dry vermouth. Simmer for approximately 3 minutes, then stir in the diced tomatoes and the broth. Incorporate the bay leaf, thyme and basil and bring to a low boil.

Remove from the heat and place the veal shanks on their side (upright). Spoon the sauce over the top of the shanks. Cover and place in the oven (make sure rack is in the center of the oven).

Bake for 11/2 to 2 hours, basting frequently with the sauce (about every 20 minutes), until the meat is very tender when tested with a fork and pulling away from the bone.

Place the veal on a platter and remove the twine. Remove the bay leaf and skim off fat from the surface. Stir the sauce and spoon over your lovely shanks. Sprinkle with parsley.

This can be made a few hours ahead; just keep the pan covered and heat on low before serving.

My Favorite Meatloaf

For years I only made turkey meatloaf, thinking that was the only way to be 'healthy' and enjoy this traditional American dish (fantastic cold the next day for sandwiches, too). I finally got bored with the poultry and switched back to lean ground beef. So it's still healthy and packed with protein. Best of all, it tastes good!

Non-stick cooking spray
2 lb (1kg) lean ground (minced) beef
1 cup (8oz, 240gm) breadcrumbs
¾ cup (6oz, 180gm) onions, chopped
1 teaspoon dried oregano
1 tablespoon prepared horseradish
1 teaspoon Dijon mustard
½ cup (4fl oz, 120ml) ketchup
2 eggs, beaten

Preheat oven to 375°F (190°C).

Spray an 8 x 4in (20 x 10cm) loaf pan with non-stick spray. In a large bowl, hand mix beef, breadcrumbs, onions, oregano, horseradish, mustard, ketchup and eggs until well incorporated.
Shape into a loaf shape and place in the pan. Bake for 1 hour.
Brush more ketchup over the top of the loaf and bake for another 15 minutes, or until a baking skewer comes out clean.

Creamy Polenta with Shiitake Mushrooms and Manchego Cheese

Here's a great dish from Amy's family files, adapted from a recipe by her grandmother, 'the polenta queen.' It serves 4–6 as a side dish.

1 cup (8oz, 240gm) stone ground yellow cornmeal (polenta)

2 cups (16fl oz, 480ml) beef broth

1 teaspoon salt

2 tablespoons white balsamic vinegar

1 tablespoon fresh thyme, minced

1 cup (8oz, 240gm) Manchego cheese, shredded

3 tablespoons extra virgin olive oil

1 shallot, minced

2 cloves garlic, minced

1 cup (8oz, 240gm) Shiitake mushrooms

¼ cup (2fl oz, 60ml) dry white wine (Sauvignon Blanc or Pinot Grigio)

Salt and freshly ground black pepper to taste

3 tablespoons fresh Italian parsley, chopped

Pour 1 cup (8fl oz, 240ml) cold water into a medium bowl, add the cornmeal and mix with a fork until smooth.

In a heavy saucepan, bring the beef broth to a boil and add the salt, along with the vinegar. Slowly pour in the cornmeal and stir constantly with a wooden spoon. If some lumps form, mash them against the side with the spoon to dissolve them. Add the fresh thyme and turn heat to low. Cook the polenta for 15–20 minutes, stirring frequently to keep smooth and from sticking to the bottom of the pot. Remove from the heat, fold in the Manchego cheese and set aside.

In a medium sauté pan, heat olive oil over medium high until haze forms. Add the minced shallot and garlic. Stir for a few seconds and then add the mushrooms. Sauté the mushrooms for approximately 1–2 minutes, while stirring frequently. Add the wine and cook for another 2 minutes. Remove from heat. Add salt and pepper to taste, along with 2 tablespoons of the parsley.

Pour the polenta into a large oval platter, top off with the mushrooms and garnish with the remaining tablespoon of chopped parsley.

Lemon Pecan Biscotti

Amy tells me, 'This is a great do-ahead recipe. Serve the biscotti with a lovely port or, better yet, some homemade Limoncello.' This recipe yields approximately 4½ dozen.

2½ cups (20oz, 600gm) pecans
3 cups (1½ lb, 700gm) unbleached all-purpose flour (plain flour)
2 teaspoons baking powder
½ teaspoon salt

3 large eggs, room temperature
1¼ cups (10oz, 300gm) sugar
5 tablespoons solid vegetable shortening, room temperature
1½ teaspoons vanilla extract

¼ teaspoon oil of lemon or 1 teaspoon lemon extract
1 teaspoon lemon extract
1 tablespoon grated lemon zest
Egg wash (beat together 1 egg and 1 teaspoon water)

Adjust your oven rack to the center and preheat to 350°F (180°C). Place the pecans on a small cookie sheet and toast until lightly golden, about 5 minutes. Transfer to a cutting board, cool slightly and coarsely chop. Set aside and leave oven on.

Line a 12 x 17in (30 x 43cm) cookie sheet with parchment paper.

In a medium bowl, combine flour, baking powder and salt. Set aside.

Place eggs, sugar and shortening in the bowl of an electric mixer. Run on medium high speed until thick and creamy, approximately 2 minutes. Add vanilla, oil of lemon (or lemon extract), grated lemon zest and blend on low speed. Add half of the dry ingredients and continue to beat on low until incorporated. Now add the rest of the dry ingredients and continue beating on low speed until the dough is crumbly and begins to mass around the beaters. Stir in pecans.

Scrape dough out onto lightly floured work surface. (This will be sticky … if it isn't, you screwed something up!) Divide dough into thirds. With lightly floured hands, shape into three ropes approximately 12in (30cm) long. Place ropes 2½in (7cm) apart on lined cookie sheet. Lightly flatten each log with your fingertips until they are ½in (1cm) high, 2in (5cm) wide and 15in (38cm) long. Brush ropes with egg wash.

Bake until logs are a deep golden color, firm to the touch and tiny cracks appear on the surface, approximately 20–25 minutes. Remove cookie sheet from the oven and place on a wire rack to cool for about 10 minutes. Lower oven temperature to 325°F (160°C).

Transfer logs to a cutting board. Leave parchment paper on cookie sheet. Using a serrated knife, gently cut logs crosswise on a slight diagonal into ½ in (1cm) slices. Place half of the slices cut side down on sheet, spacing them ½in (1cm) apart. Return pan to oven and bake until surfaces are lightly toasted, about 7–8 minutes on each side. Transfer the biscotti to a wire rack and cool completely.

Limoncello

The first time I'd seen Amy after a few years' separation, she brought along an amazing treat: the last bottle of Limoncello her late mother had ever made. What a special, personal gift it was for her to share with me. And we drank every delicious drop!

Now, as a special gift to you, Amy presents that lip-smacking recipe so you can share it with people you love! She says that, while it's simple to make, 'it's the waiting that's the hard part! It needs to steep for eighty days.' But take heart … 'All good things take time,' Amy chides. 'I usually make a double batch so that I can bottle it and use it as hostess gifts.'

2 x 750ml (26fl oz) bottles of good quality 100 proof vodka (must be 100 proof; so the Limoncello won't turn to ice in the freezer)
15 large thick-skinned lemons
4 cups (2lb, 950gm) sugar
Mint sprigs

Pour one bottle of vodka into a large glass jar with a lid.

Wash the lemons in hot water with a vegetable brush to ensure the removal of any waxy residue or pesticides. Pat them dry and remove the zest with a vegetable peeler.
This works best as it gives you nice long strips. Scrape any white pith from the peels with a knife and drop the peels into the jar. Cover the jar with the lid and place it in a dark cabinet or closet at room temperature. Wait forty days. Mark your calendar!

After forty days, combine the sugar and 5 cups (2½ pints, 1.2 L) water together in a saucepan and bring to a low boil. Stir until thickened, approximately 5–7 minutes.
Let the syrup cool completely, then add it to the jar with the lemon peels and vodka.
Pour in the second bottle of vodka and return the jar to its secret hiding place for another forty days.

Go away and come back later …

After eighty days, open the jar and discard the lemon peels. Strain into bottles.
Store the bottles in a cool dark space but always keep a few in the freezer so that you can be 'Limoncello ready'! Serve either straight up or over cracked ice, and garnish with a sprig of mint.

Ruta Lee

Richard Quest

Sunrise Specials

Dinner with

Ruta Lee
Richard Quest

Menu

Walnut Baguette Rounds
or
Curried Carrot Dip
Garlic Baked Chicken
or
Philly Cheese Steak Sandwiches
Mel's Fruit Crumble
or
Sunrise Family Scones

Suggested Wine

Bardolino, a lighter bodied red from Northern Italy

Two of the most colorful personalities I know are Ruta Lee and Richard Quest. And while they both live and work in very opposite ends of the broadcast world, they are similarly energetic and delightful company.

Ruta (born Ruta Mary Kilmonis in Montreal, Quebec, to Lithuanian immigrant parents) came to Hollywood in 1948 and worked as an usherette and candy girl at the famous Grauman's Chinese Theater before getting her big break on TV with the legendary George Burns and Gracie Allen. A successful film career followed soon after, and she landed roles in many famous films including *Seven Brides For Seven Brothers*, *Anything Goes*, *Funny Face*, *Witness for The Prosecution* and *Marjorie Morningstar*, playing opposite some of the biggest stars in movie history. In the 1970s and 80s, I grew up watching her many guest-starring roles on TV series and game shows. Modern audiences remember her hysterical work on *Roseanne*, playing the 'lipstick lesbian' girlfriend of Roseanne's mom, Bev (Estelle Parsons). A renowned human rights activist, Ruta has the distinction of having arranged rescues for relatives in the former Soviet Union (going all the way to Nikita Khruschev!) and for more than a half-century has worked tirelessly for Hollywood's esteemed 'Thalians' philanthropic organization, alongside fellow film luminary Debbie Reynolds ... another dandy dame I've had the pleasure of knowing for years. She's one of the most cherished stars we have and, wonderfully, her 'star' on the Walk of Fame is right in front of her teenage stomping grounds: the Chinese Theater.

Anyone who's ever caught CNN knows my mate Richard Quest. Even the network's own public relations team refers to him as 'instantly recognizable', and that's primarily because of his frenetic energy, larger than life persona

Since 1955, the Thalians organization has been doing philanthropic work in the Los Angeles community and even has a Mental Health Center at the famed Cedars Sinai Hospital named for them. They continue to raise over $500,000 annually through events and fundraisers. Ruta's determination to integrate young showbiz types to get involved and carry on their great legacy is one of her driving passions.

and obvious intelligence. An expert in the fields of business and travel, he's as captivating on camera reporting hard news stories like the death of Pope John Paul II and the Iraq War as he is amusing in his coverage of the Concorde's last flight and talking to 'the man on the street.' His unique ability to be both informative and entertaining is an inspiration to all of us in the TV presenting world. We actually met initially via satellite. Based in England, he'd be watching me report from Hollywood to the UK morning show, GMTV, while I'd be watching him on CNN's overnight news broadcast. A few emails later, a friendship was born! We've had the fun of catching up for tea in London, breakfast in Los Angeles and even hanging out at Julie Andrews' suite in Manhattan. In the wonderful world of broadcast journalism, it's always a fortunate coincidence when we bump into each other covering events like the Oscars or Michael Jackson's funeral.

After a half-century of annual Thalians' Galas presided over by Ruta and Debbie Reynolds, she admits they are her most memorable dinner parties and 'always super-star-studded events' with the likes of Whoopi Goldberg, Sally Field, Mickey Rooney, Angelina Jolie, Shirley MacLaine and many others. Who says doing good deeds is hard work?! 'You can brighten a saddened heart with a glowing smile. That, too, is charitable in God's eyes,' she reminds us.

Richard, although he primarily covers 'hard' news, balks at the suggestion that he considers showbiz assignments journalistic 'slumming'. 'No!' he loudly protests to me. 'The exact opposite! You guys get to do that fun, interesting stuff all the time. I could argue that it's not curing poverty or AIDS, but for twenty-five years I've talked about bloody interest rates and sometimes, it's just nice to talk about sex and tits. I'm jealous of my colleagues who get to do Entertainment stories.' So his response might not surprise you when I asked him who'd be his dream dinner party companions: 'Absolutely the Queen. After that it would be Tom Cruise. He might be a few sandwiches short of a picnic. But if I could have Her Royal Highness on one side and Tom Cruise on the other, I think we would have an amazing time.'

Ruta's response also melded Hollywood with Jolly Olde England. 'My dream dinner party dates would be Margaret Thatcher with Clint Eastwood.' Saucily she adds, 'Come to think of it … I already had Clint Eastwood.'

As I mentioned, Ruta's been working in show business for generations and, in addition to keeping her good looks and great humor, she's managed to avoid any scandals and other publicity nightmares that seem to plague 'young Hollywood.' I asked her to reflect on what the difference is these days and she had a quick comeback. 'With due credit to Dr Spock, the now generation is a me, me, me generation! Very few of the younger ones are interested in sharing their blessings—either by paying back or forward.' Was it her tremendous work ethic that kept her out of trouble? 'I thank my Lithuanian-born parents,' she says, 'who came to the new world and with hard work lived the "American Dream."' And yes, Ruta speaks fluent Lithuanian!

She also has enjoyed a happy marriage of over thirty years ... another rarity in the entertainment industry. She and Webster Lowe, Jr, were married on Valentine's Day in 1976 and are still going strong. Their secret: 'Disagreements should never become fights. Through my husband, I adopted a credo: will your bone of contention be important in five minutes? An hour? A day? A week? Or a year? It's a waste of time, energy and life to stew over nothing.'

But the best career advice she ever got was from her 'non-showbiz' mother: 'Whatever you do, do with your whole heart.'

And what life lessons did Richard learn as he started on his career path? 'My late father once told me, "The problem with being a journalist, Richard, is that you will have the best dinner party stories and the smallest car parked outside."'

(L-R): The Unsinkable Ruta Lee! Taking Melissa Doyle and her family to their first Dodgers game ... and meeting the legendary manager, Joe Torre! Richard Quest, one of TV's most talented.

Walnut Baguette Rounds

1 baguette
2 cups (16 oz, 480gm) walnuts
2 cups (16 oz, 480gm) Parmesan, grated
1 teaspoon kosher salt
2 tablespoons lemon juice
⅔ cup (5fl oz, 140ml) olive oil

Thinly slice the baguette into rounds and place on a baking sheet.
Broil about a minute on each side, until golden brown.

In food processor, pulse walnuts, Parmesan (save a little for garnishing), and salt until crumbly.
While still pulsing, slowly add lemon juice and the oil in a slow, steady stream.

Spread the mixture onto the rounds and garnish with extra Parmesan.

Curried Carrot Dip

This tangy, tasty dip is quick and easy to prepare and delicious on crudités like carrots, celery or red peppers. Also very nice with plain water biscuits.

⅓ cup (2½oz, 70gm) fresh carrots, finely grated
2 cups (16fl oz, 480ml) light sour cream
2 tablespoons apricot preserves
1 tablespoon prepared yellow mustard
4 teaspoons curry powder
½ to l teaspoon bottled crumbled red chili flakes

Mix all ingredients well together and serve.

Garlic Baked Chicken

1 whole chicken
1 lemon
1 cup (8oz, 240gm) unsalted butter, softened
3 tablespoons garlic, minced
¼ cup (2oz, 60gm) chopped fresh rosemary
Salt and black pepper to taste
1 teaspoon paprika
5 cloves garlic, sliced
5 sprigs fresh rosemary

- -

Preheat oven to 350°F (180°C).

Rinse chicken and pat dry with paper towels. Zest the lemon.
Slice remaining lemon into quarters and put aside.

Combine butter, zest, minced garlic and chopped rosemary. Scoop up some of the butter mixture and rub into the bird and between the legs and wings, saving a quarter of the mixture.

Season the cavity of the chicken with the salt, pepper and paprika.
Then add the quartered lemon, rosemary sprigs and sliced garlic to the chicken cavity.
Tie the legs with twine and secure the wings into the leg joints.

Place the chicken breast-side-up on the roasting rack and roast for approximately 50 minutes, or until the juices run clear. Remove the lemon slices, rosemary sprigs and garlic slices from the cavity. Carve and serve.

Philly Cheese Steak Sandwiches

I grew up just outside of Philadelphia where cheese steak sandwiches have long been a part of the culture. There are all sorts of variations on the South Philly classic, so whether you're a Rocky Balboa or a Grace Kelly, it's most certainly an inescapable, in-bred craving!

Depending on the size of your skillet or griddle, you may need to split this recipe in half and prepare in two batches.

¼ cup (2fl oz, 60ml) olive oil

2 white onions, thinly sliced

1 large green bell pepper (capsicum), thinly sliced

2 teaspoons garlic, minced

1 teaspoon salt

1/2 teaspoon black pepper

1 lb (450gm) rib-eye steak, thinly shaved or sliced (as thin as you can possibly slice!)

1¼ cups (9½oz, 270gm) thinly sliced white 'American' cheese. If not available, use provolone.

4 fresh Italian sandwich ('hoagie') rolls

Optional dressings:

Ketchup, Italian peppers, sautéed button mushrooms

- -

Heat the oil in a large skillet over medium–high heat. When hot, add onions and bell peppers and stir until caramelized, about 5–6 minutes. Add garlic, salt and pepper, and continue stirring until well mixed. Push off to the side of the skillet.

Add the meat to the hot pan and cook, tenderizing with the back of a metal spatula, until no longer pink (2–3 minutes). Mix with the vegetables. Top with cheese slices.

As soon as the cheese has melted into a gooey mixture, spoon a portion into roll and serve immediately. A sandwich fit for a Philadelphia King!

Mel's Fruit Crumble

For over seven years, I've had the pleasure of chatting live every weekday on Australian television with my 'satellite sister', Melissa Doyle. She's one of that country's most treasured and beloved on-air personalities and I can vouch for the fact that she's just as wonderful offscreen.

She also happens to be a yummy-mummy in the kitchen! I've enjoyed several of her delightful dishes while visiting her Sydney home and here's a dessert she 'borrowed' from Jamie Oliver and then cleverly personalized. It's easy and delish!

Crumble

1½ cups (12oz, 350gm) plain flour
3 tablespoons butter
1 cup (8oz, 240gm) brown sugar
Any of the following depending on your taste:
rolled oats, cashew nuts, macadamia nuts, almonds.

Fruit filling

1 lb (500gm, 2 cups) fruit of choice (Mel recommends peaches, apricots, plums, pears or apples with raisins)
3 tablespoons brown sugar

- -

Preheat oven to 350°F (180°C).

Chop the fruit and toss it all in an oven-safe dish.
Whiz the crumble mix in a food processor then sprinkle on top.

Bake for 30 minutes. Serve with a big dollop of ice cream.

Sunrise Family Scones

The lovely newsreader for Australia's Sunrise morning show, Natalie Barr, has been a friend since we first met on location in Las Vegas way back in 2004. She's not only very professional and trustworthy in her role as journalist, but she is devilishly wry and witty when it comes to matters other than news. She's also very popular for her baking skills. I asked her for a recipe and she gave me her mum's for scones. But I had to get her to be specific with her measurements and temperature criteria ... she's definitely of the 'old school', with a pinch of this and dash of that.

However, after two failed attempts at her 'three-ingredient' recipe (flour, cream, water), all I was left with was a messy kitchen and burned up batter that even the dog rejected! When I mentioned it (off-camera) to Nat the next day, we hypothesized that something must've gotten lost in translation from metric to imperial but I suspect it was the difference in Aussie versus American flours. During a live report that same day, our show host Melissa Doyle couldn't resist bringing up my scone debacle as an unexpected ad lib and we wound up in a hilarious 'How-To' chat that sent thousands of Australian morning TV viewers into a frenzy of recipe sharing.

In the end, we combined Nat's version with some of the more popular viewers' methods and I enlisted my darling mother as a test chef until we came up with the best 'intercontinental' version, which is below. Sometimes, to create a globally viable recipe, you need a lot of chefs in the kitchen!

These are a nice alternative to traditional dinner rolls, or you can serve them with whipped or clotted cream and a sweet jam for dessert. Whatever you decide, cross your fingers ... just in case.

4 cups (2lb, 950gm) self-raising flour (not 'all purpose')
1¼ cup (10fl oz, 300ml) cream
1¼ cup (10fl oz, 300ml) 7-Up soda (called 'Lemonade' in Australia)
2 teaspoons baking powder
Pinch of salt

- -

Preheat oven to 400°F (200°C).

Sift flour into a bowl. Add cream and 7-Up, and mix gently with a knife.
Add baking powder and salt and mix to combine.

Pat together and spread out onto a floured cutting board, about an inch thick.
Use a glass to cut out into rounds (big or small), then place on oven tray so rounds are touching.

Bake for about 10–15 minutes or until slightly brown on top. (My mom swears that '14 and a half minutes is great'.) Remove from oven and wrap in a dish towel. Cool slightly.

Cut in half and top with jam and cream!

That's a Wrap!

Just as all good dinner parties must come to an end, so must this book. It's been a genuine pleasure sharing the company of my showbiz friends with you. I hope you found them to be as charming and entertaining on the printed page (or e-book, if that's how you're reading this) as I find them in three dimensions!

Hopefully, you'll try your hand at some of the recipes and let me know how they turn out. Nothing's foolproof, but I think you should find success and satisfaction with any you whip up in your own kitchen. Be sure to invite friends and loved ones to be your taste-testers. No matter how good a meal is, it's always much more delicious when it's shared.

While you can easily find me on the internet through my website (www.nelsonaspen.com) and Twitter page (www.twitter.com/nelsonaspen), I hope if you decide to drop me a line it will be via 'snail mail'. I'm a big fan of the lost art of letter writing and greatly welcome the arrival of the postman! You may write to me c/o New Holland Publishing.

I wish you a life filled with love and laughter, abundant blessings, juicy dishes and delicious dinner parties!

Nelson Aspen,
Hollywood and New York City

Acknowledgements

It's impossible to put together a book like this without the generous contributions of 'cuisine and conversation' given to me by all the fabulous folks you've met in these pages. As Auntie Mame famously said, 'Life is a banquet and most poor sons-of-bitches are starving to death!' My life is a smorgasbord of terrific people and they are definitely my sustenance!

There are also plenty of people 'behind the scenes' whose support and camaraderie made this a labor of love. The talented team at New Holland Publishers continues to make the process of writing, publishing and promoting my books pure pleasure. My Aussie manager, Matt Clarke, has become like a brother to me, especially over the last tumultuous year. In addition to Matt, my US agent, John Derr, makes the 'business' part of 'show business' much easier to navigate. No one is closer to me than my best friend, Glenn, who continues to make my bi-coastal life between Hollywood and Manhattan one giant adventure.

Special thanks, too, to Kaore and Steve, the Forbes family, my friends in the Seven Network Los Angeles Bureau, Ireland's RTE, the Kiwis' TVNZ, Pacific Television, ME Management, Air New Zealand and all my Twitter followers.

My dog, Lois, passed away during the writing of this book. My constant companion for nearly 16 years, she was the heartbeat of my home and the happiest component of every dinner party I ever hosted there.